The Art of Balancing Relationships

RELATIONSHIP ADVICE FOR WOMEN

FOR WOMEN

IN LOVE TRIANGLES:

How to Get Over Infidelity and Save or End Your
Marriage with Confidence

CONTENTS

WHY THIS BOOK?

A Woman in a Love Triangle Who Is Being Cheated on – the second book in the series *The Art of Balancing Relationships.*

This book was created for women who have faced betrayal from their partner in long-term relationships or marriage.

Love is one of the most powerful emotions, capable of both bringing happiness and causing destruction. This is especially evident in situations where feelings are intertwined with infidelity, betrayal, and insecurity. When a woman finds herself in a love triangle and faces her man's betrayal, the world seems turned upside down. Every action, every word takes on new meaning, and the heart breaks from pain and disappointment.

This book will help you:

- Understand why men have affairs.

- Provide step-by-step strategies on how to cope with the pain of betrayal.

- Help you decide whether to forgive, leave, or eliminate the mistress.

- Provide clarity on which types of infidelity can be forgiven and which cannot.

- Teach you how to trust again. You will receive strategies for strengthening trust in relationships.

- Learn effective practical steps for ending a relationship.

This book is intended for those who are going through such a difficult stage in their life. It will help you navigate the complex and often painful issues related to love triangles, infidelity, and rebuilding trust in relationships. In the first chapter, we will examine the reasons why men have affairs, the factors that affect their loyalty, and how to avoid infidelity in relationships. We will also talk about the importance of a woman's self-esteem and how low self-esteem can destroy even the strongest relationships.

In the second chapter, we will explore reactions and strategies for dealing with infidelity. What to do when you catch your man cheating. How to survive the first days after betrayal. We will provide step-by-step instructions on how to cope with the pain, restore your inner balance, and decide whether or not to save the family.

The third chapter is dedicated to the important and difficult choice — whether to forgive infidelity, leave, or fight for the relationship. We will give you tools to make your decision, explain how to get your man back from the mistress, and what steps will help you restore the family. We will also examine which types of infidelity can be forgiven and which are unforgivable.

In the fourth chapter, we will focus on rebuilding trust. After infidelity, a woman often loses faith not only in her man but also in herself. How to regain trust, how to learn to love and trust again, how to rebuild a relationship after betrayal — these are the questions we will offer you concrete answers and recommendations for.

Finally, in the fifth chapter, we will discuss how to end a relationship when it no longer has a future. We will suggest practical steps for making the decision to part ways with minimal suffering and open yourself up to new, healthy relationships.

You need the first book in *The Art of Balancing Relationships* series: *How to Deal With a Love Triangle* if you are interested in topics such as:

- Three in One Story: Mental Roots of Love Triangles.

- Why Does a Third Person Appear in a Relationship?

- What Do Men and Women Want? Key Needs in Relationships.

- Forgive or Leave: How to Make the Right Decision After Infidelity.

- How to Make a Relationship Choice: Five Strategies for Conscious Decision-Making.

- Seven Ways to Exit a Love Triangle.

Infidelity, betrayal, and love triangles are tough trials, but they can be a starting point for personal growth and restoring inner harmony. This book will help you go through these trials, understand your feelings, and find the right path for yourself. You deserve happiness, love, and harmony in your relationships. And this book will be your assistant on the way to these goals.

CHAPTER 1.

WHY MEN HAVE AFFAIRS

Male infidelity is a painful, complicated, and often silenced topic. What drives a man to betrayal? Is it always the woman's fault? Or are there much deeper psychological, emotional, and social reasons behind it?

In this chapter, we will discuss:

- Thirteen key factors that lead men to cheat, and what to do to protect your family.

- Simple steps to harmony that help strengthen loyalty.

- How low self-esteem interferes with love and destroys relationships and how to raise it using 5 proven methods.

- Why even the most beautiful women are cheated on, and the 4 hidden factors behind it.

- And most importantly, 7 mistakes that prevent a woman from building truly happy and trusting relationships.

It is time to uncover the truth and stop suffering in silence. We can figure it out together.

WHY DO MEN CHEAT? 13 FACTORS AND WAYS TO PROTECT YOUR FAMILY FROM INFIDELITY

Infidelity in marriage is an issue that many couples face. According to statistics, 75% of men have cheated on their wives, but only 5% of women found out about it. This does not mean that all marriages are doomed, but it does make us reflect on the reasons behind marital infidelity.

Why does infidelity cause so much pain? Why does infidelity destroy a marriage and intimacy in an instant? What exactly breaks down? What happens to us in that moment? Why, even if the marriage survives after infidelity, does the pain not leave us years later?

The institution of marriage in the modern world has become more flexible: There are same-sex marriages and other forms of partnerships. But infidelity remains an unchanging part of these relationships. The modern world has become more sexually active: People used to marry and have sex for the first time, but now they marry after many romances and experiences. Marriage has become a conscious choice to limit sexual freedom and a demonstration of serious intent. Fidelity now symbolizes importance and devotion.

Monogamy says: "You are not just chosen, you are the only one." And infidelity sounds like: "You are just like everyone else, you are one of many." That is why the pain of infidelity is so intense — it is the pain of rejection. From childhood, we are wired with the fear of being rejected because a child's rejection threatens their survival. We need a strong connection, just like

9

we did with our parents when we were children. Infidelity destroys two key internal beliefs: first, that your marriage is unique and secure, and second, that you are valuable and chosen by your partner.

Why Do People Cheat?

In culture, a paradox has strengthened: on one hand, the desire for exclusivity, and on the other, the thirst for pleasure, consumption, and the fear of missing out on opportunities. The reason for infidelity today is not the partner's flaws, but the desire to experience more: new relationships, sex, emotions. Everything around stimulates: "live now," "achieve by 20," "make a million." This activity creates weakness and instability in marriage.

So why do men, who once promised to be faithful, later have affairs? We can look at the key factors.

1. **Sexual attraction and physiological differences.** One of the main reasons for male infidelity is the difference in sexual desire between men and women. Men's sexual desire remains relatively stable over time, while women's desire fluctuates depending on their hormonal cycle, fatigue, and other factors.

In relationships, a situation often arises where a woman, for various objective reasons, begins to refuse intimacy: fatigue, caring for a child, stress at work. In this case, the man may resort to self-pleasure or watching pornography, but over time, he may think, "Why did I get married if I have to do this alone?" This leads to disappointment and emotional distance from his partner.

2. **The influence of the external environment and the informational background.** Modern men are constantly influenced by content that creates the illusion of the availability of sex. Watching porn, communicating on social media, and participating in male forums create the sense that women, in general, are more open to intimacy than one's own wife.

Moreover, in the early months of a relationship, women often show sexual activity, but then the level of passion decreases. This leads to the man feeling deceived: "Sex used to be regular and passionate, but now it is almost nonexistent." Against this background, the temptation to enter into a relationship with another woman who shows him attention and interest arises.

3. **Feeling of being unnecessary in the family.** One of the main reasons for infidelity is the feeling that a man has stopped being important to his wife. When a man comes home and does not receive basic attention, he feels isolated. If his requests or complaints are met with indifferent responses like "Figure it out yourself," "I don't have time," "I take care of everything," over time, this leads to internal alienation.

When a man is seen solely as a source of income or as someone who is responsible for household duties (driving the children, fixing things around the house, helping relatives), but there is no emotional connection in the couple, he starts seeking affirmation of his significance elsewhere.

4. **Mismatch of temperaments and sexual dissatisfaction.** Different levels of sexual desire in a relationship can lead to growing tension. If, at the beginning of the relationship, sex was

frequent and emotionally charged, but later became rare and mechanical, the man starts feeling a lack of closeness.

The problem is further amplified by the fact that there are always temptations around him: colleagues, social media, casual acquaintances who flirt and make it clear that they are open to relationships. If his desires are ignored at home, but outside he receives attention and seductive glances, the risk of infidelity increases.

5.   **Emotional discomfort and lack of care.** When there is no warmth in a relationship, and the woman shows rudeness, sarcasm, or passive-aggressive behavior, the man feels overwhelmed. If a man does not feel cozy and comfortable at home, it may push him to seek emotional and physical warmth elsewhere.

The combination of these factors leads to alienation: The man does not feel needed, there is no intimate closeness in the relationship, and the wife stops considering his emotions and desires. As a result, he seeks an outlet in new relationships.

6.   **Refusal of intimate life during pregnancy and after childbirth.** Pregnancy and childbirth are challenging periods that require a lot of strength and attention. However, a complete exclusion of intimacy for a long period can lead to distance between the spouses.

What happens? The woman distances herself from her husband, focusing solely on her condition. Sexual life completely stops, sometimes for up to a year. The man remains without physical closeness, which can affect his emotional state and push him to seek warmth elsewhere.

How to avoid the problem? Even if traditional sex is impossible for medical reasons, it is important to maintain physical and emotional closeness. Show care, attention, and discuss your feelings and needs.

7.   **Complete immersion in motherhood.** After the birth of a child, some women completely shift their focus to the role of motherhood, forgetting about the marital relationship.

What happens? The woman stops paying attention to her husband. She constantly sleeps with the child, excluding the husband from this process. Breastfeeding lasts 3–5 years without considering the husband's needs.

What are the consequences? The man feels unnecessary and emotionally distant. Sexual life gradually fades. The temptation to compensate for the lack of warmth and attention elsewhere arises.

How to avoid the problem? Remember that family is not just about the child, but also the relationship between husband and wife. It is important to find a balance between motherhood and marital life.

8.   **Breakdowns in relationships due to quarrels.** Some women, when in conflict with their husbands, resort to radical measures: They kick him out of the house, pack their things, and go to their parents or friends. They stop talking, staging a boycott.

What are the consequences? The man begins to feel unnecessary. He gradually gets used to living without his wife, losing emotional attachment to her. He may seek comfort elsewhere.

Conflicts should be resolved constructively, without destroying trust and creating distance.

9.   **Manipulation with sex.** A woman may use intimacy as a tool for punishment: refusing sex as revenge, waiting for him to beg. She may drag out the period of absence of intimacy for a long time.

What does this lead to? The man feels frustration and dissatisfaction. He starts looking for alternative ways to fulfill his needs. He may have an affair. Sexual life is important for relationships. Instead of manipulation, it is better to discuss the reasons for misunderstandings and find a compromise.

10.   **Stopping working together.** If the couple met and started their relationship at work, after the wife leaves her job, the man may feel the lack of her attention.

Why is this important? Working together provided constant interaction. The man was used to having his wife in his work environment. After she leaves her job, the woman falls out of this part of his life. If the relationship began in a work environment, it is important to maintain contact and interest in the spouse's life, even if you no longer work together.

11.   **Refusal to wear the wedding ring.** In some families, spouses stop wearing their wedding rings, explaining it with various reasons:

- The ring is tight or uncomfortable.
- They do not like the appearance.
- It gets in the way of work.
- Allergies to metal.

How does this affect the relationship? The absence of a ring may be perceived by others as a signal of being free. This increases interest from the opposite sex and raises the likelihood of flirting.

12.   **Sudden changes in the husband's appearance.** When a man suddenly starts paying more attention to his appearance — taking care of himself, going to the gym, changing his clothing style — it could indicate a desire to make an impression.

What could this be caused by?

- The desire to feel young and attractive again.

- Receiving attention from other women.

- Feeling undervalued in the family.

If the wife does not show interest in the changes her husband makes, while other women compliment him, it may push him toward infidelity.

13.   **Lack of transparency in financial matters.** Some women do not know how much their husband earns or how he manages money. The absence of financial transparency may lead to the wife not noticing if a mistress enters his life. It is important to discuss the family budget and understand income and expenses so that potential warning signs are not overlooked.

Male infidelity is not always a story about love for another woman. Most often, it stems from unmet needs, a lack of closeness, recognition, sexual contact, and emotional warmth in the marriage. It becomes a consequence of distance, resentments, household overloads, and unspoken expectations. Understanding the causes is the first step to protecting your relationship from betrayal. It is easier to prevent infidelity than to heal from it. That is why it is important to notice warning signs in time, be attentive to yourself and your partner, communicate with each other, and work on trust, mutual attraction, and inner resilience.

HOW TO AVOID INFIDELITY? SIMPLE STEPS TO FIDELITY AND HARMONY IN RELATIONSHIPS

How to avoid cooling off in a relationship? Maintaining passion requires conscious efforts from both partners. Key recommendations:

- **Set aside time for intimacy.** Sex is not just a spontaneous act, but an activity that requires planning. A regular intimate life is important for maintaining an emotional connection in the relationship.

- **Create the right atmosphere.** It is important that sex does not turn into mechanical actions before sleep. Beautiful lingerie, music, and a pleasant environment help to diversify intimacy and make it desirable for both partners.

- **Change the environment.** Sometimes it is worth stepping outside the usual scenario: plan a meeting at a hotel, retreat to a separate apartment, or organize an unexpected romantic evening.

- **Emotional closeness.** Often, the lack of sex is not due to physiology, but the lack of warmth in the relationship. It is important to talk to each other, support your partner, and spend leisure time together.

- **Financial investment in the relationship.** When a man spends money on his wife's pleasures — gifts, treatments, little joys — it creates a sense of value and recognition for her, which positively affects intimacy.

Can infidelity be avoided?

Infidelity does not always mean the end of a marriage. It is important to realize that problems in a relationship begin long before infidelity. To prevent cooling off and maintain the connection, it is crucial to:

- Maintain emotional closeness, show interest in each other's thoughts and feelings.

- Talk about your needs and seek compromises.

- Regularly devote time to your intimate life, understanding that sex is not just physiology, but a way to strengthen the connection.

- Demonstrate care and respect, creating an atmosphere in which your partner feels valued.

In my book, *The Simple Formula for Communication,* I explain how to engage in healthy dialogue, how to identify each partner's needs, and how to express anger constructively. I highly recommend reading it and applying my simple four-step communication formula.

Healthy relationships require attention and investment from both sides. Awareness, the willingness to work on the relationship, and openness to each other help avoid infidelity and strengthen the bond. Strong relationships are built not only on love but also on a conscious approach to intimacy. Regularity, attention to each other's needs, and emotional connection are key factors that help avoid cooling off in the relationship and maintain harmony.

How can a wife unintentionally provoke her husband into infidelity? In family relationships, situations often arise where one partner feels a lack of an important aspect of the marriage. One frequent example is a lack of intimacy, which can lead to what is called "compensatory infidelity."

A real-life story

In one family, a woman found out that her husband had been having an affair for two years. He had no intention of leaving the family, did not invest significant resources into the new relationship, and did not have serious plans. According to him, the mistress served only one purpose — compensating for the lack of intimacy in the marriage.

The woman confessed that she had often told her husband in anger, "Find yourself a mistress, leave me alone." For her, it was just an irritated remark, but for her husband, it became a sort of permission to seek the missing intimacy outside the marriage.

What is compensatory infidelity?

Compensatory infidelity happens when a person is happy with their marriage but feels the lack of one important aspect — sexual, emotional, or domestic closeness. Instead of addressing the problem within the family, they "fill in" the missing element elsewhere, trying not to get too attached and not destroy the family.

In the story, the man's mistress was also married, but her husband showed no interest in intimacy, so she compensated for this shortfall through extramarital relations.

How to avoid such situations?

- **Pay attention to your partner's needs.** If one aspect of the relationship no longer satisfies your spouse, it is important not to ignore the problem but to look for solutions together.

- **Avoid sharp phrases during arguments.** Phrases like "Get yourself a mistress," "I do not have time for you," or "I do not care about this" can be taken literally and eventually lead to a crisis in the marriage.

- **Regularly discuss the relationship.** An honest conversation about needs, desires, and expectations helps avoid the buildup of mutual resentments and misunderstandings.

- **Work on intimacy.** Relationships require attention and investment from both partners. Maintaining physical and emotional closeness is an important element of a long-term partnership.

Compensatory infidelity arises when spouses stop noticing each other's needs. To avoid such situations, it is important to recognize dissatisfaction signals in time, maintain open dialogue, and seek joint solutions.

In the first book about love triangles, you can find detailed instructions to prevent infidelity. The book includes chapters such as "Fidelity in the Modern World: 6 Effective Strategies Against Infidelity" and "When You are Tempted to Cheat: What to Do If You Want to Be Unfaithful?"

WHY LOW SELF-ESTEEM INTERFERES WITH LOVE: HOW IT AFFECTS RELATIONSHIPS WITH MEN

A woman's self-esteem plays a key role in building harmonious relationships. How a woman perceives herself influences her behavior, choice of partner, and emotional comfort in relationships.

Consequences of Low Self-Esteem

1.   **Fear of Loneliness and Dependence on a Partner**. A woman with low self-esteem often fears being alone and, therefore, clings to any man who pays attention to her. In such a state, she may be willing to tolerate inappropriate relationships just to avoid being alone.

2.   **High Probability of Manipulation**. Men who tend to dominate or use their partner for their own purposes quickly sense the woman's weaknesses. She may become a victim of gold-diggers, tyrants, or emotionally cold partners who exploit her desire to earn love.

3.   **Unconscious Desire to Keep a Man Through Pregnancy**. A woman may make impulsive decisions, such as trying to keep a man with a child, believing that this will strengthen the relationship. However, such unions rarely become strong, and the consequences can be complex and painful.

4.   **Suppression of Her Own Desires and Needs**. A woman with low self-esteem often puts her partner's interests above her own. She is afraid to express her opinion, fears rejection, and

gradually loses her personal boundaries. This leads to the accumulation of resentment, exhaustion, and disappointment.

Dangers of Excessively High Self-Esteem. The flip side of the problem is inflated self-esteem. A woman who sees herself as a "queen" may wait for the "perfect" man, rejecting everyone who does not meet her inflated standards. As a result, she may miss the chance for a healthy relationship and end up alone.

How to Form Adequate Self-Esteem?

- **Work on Yourself**. It is important to understand your strengths and weaknesses and work on what can be improved: appearance, knowledge, and communication skills.

- **An Objective View of Yourself**. Healthy self-esteem is a balance between accepting yourself and striving for development. A woman should see her strengths and weaknesses but not obsess over them.

- **Harmonious Relationship with Yourself**. Developing confidence, self-sufficiency, and inner comfort helps build healthy relationships where a woman values herself and chooses a worthy partner.

- **Psychological Support**. If it is difficult to deal with insecurity on your own, you can turn to a specialist or study psychological literature that helps you view yourself objectively.

Adequate self-esteem is the foundation of happy and healthy relationships. A woman who knows her worth does not cling to unworthy relationships, does not allow herself to be manipulated, and consciously chooses a partner. This gives her the chance for long-lasting and harmonious love.

5 PROVEN WAYS FOR A WOMAN TO BOOST HER SELF-ESTEEM AND BECOME CONFIDENT

A woman's self-esteem largely determines the quality of her life and relationships. It affects self-confidence, partner choice, and the ability to accept love and attention. We can break down the key points that can help eliminate insecurities and strengthen confidence.

1.   **Work on Your Appearance**. How you feel about yourself is often reflected through your outward appearance. When a woman takes care of herself, she not only looks better but also feels more valuable.

- **Self-care** – Investing time and resources in your appearance helps raise self-esteem.

- **Grooming as stress relief** – A well-groomed appearance helps you feel more confident and reduces anxiety.

- **Social feedback** – People perceive women differently based on their appearance. When a woman is well-groomed and stylish, she receives more positive reactions, which positively impacts her self-esteem.

It is important to remember that appearance is not only about looks but also behavior. If a person looks attractive but behaves withdrawn and insecure, others may perceive this as a barrier to communication.

2.   **Openness and Nonverbal Behavior.**

- **Straight posture and confident gaze** – Confident people walk with their heads held high, demonstrating openness to the world.

- **Eye contact** – Looking into someone's eyes during conversation shows confidence and engagement.

- **Expressive facial expressions and friendliness** – A smile and an open expression make a person more attractive to others.

Openness in communication helps to receive more positive attention and strengthens the sense of self-importance.

3. **Influence of Society and Criticism**. People are social beings, and the opinions of others influence self-esteem. However, it is important to differentiate between constructive criticism and subjective remarks.

- **Taste-based criticism** – This reflects the preferences of the critic and has no relation to your personality. It is not worth focusing on.

- **Expert criticism** – Advice from people who have achieved success in a particular area. Such remarks should be seen as an opportunity for growth.

Women with low self-esteem often react painfully to any criticism, taking it as truth. It is important to learn how to separate useful advice from irrelevant comments.

4. **Influence of Environment.**

- **Support from significant people** – Self-esteem strengthens when there are people around who appreciate and respect you.

- **Development of hobbies** – It is important to have a hobby or activity that brings pleasure and fosters a sense of self-fulfillment.

- **Balance in relationships** – Love is built on mutual exchange, not on sacrifice. A woman should give her partner as much as she wants, not try to earn his attention.

5. Inner Comfort and Self-Acceptance. Increasing self-esteem is not only about working on appearance and behavior, but also an internal process.

- **Awareness of your value** – It is important to understand that self-esteem should not only depend on the opinions of others.

- **Flexibility in development** – Adequate self-esteem means the ability to work on yourself while accepting your strengths and weaknesses.

A woman who is confident in herself does not cling to other people's opinions, is not afraid to express her desires, and builds relationships as equals. This is what makes her truly attractive.

WHY DO EVEN THE MOST BEAUTIFUL WOMEN GET CHEATED ON? 4 FACTORS THAT AFFECT LOYALTY

A woman's beauty is not a guarantee of her partner's fidelity. Even the most attractive wives face infidelity, and there are several common reasons for this.

1.   **Lack or Insufficiency of Intimacy.** A man may be proud of his wife's beauty, but if there is no sex in the relationship for a long time, this can lead to seeking satisfaction elsewhere.

If the wife shows no interest in intimacy – if the husband regularly faces rejection or if intimacy becomes rare and formal, his dissatisfaction builds up.

The mistress may be less attractive – appearance here plays a secondary role. What matters is not only how a woman looks but also how she is in terms of intimacy, how open, active, and ready to experiment she is.

2.   **Conservatism and Monotony in Sex.** Beauty cannot compensate for the lack of emotional or physical passion in intimacy.

- If the wife sticks to strict boundaries – if there is monotony in sex, the man may look for variety elsewhere.

- Sexual dissatisfaction – even with the most beautiful wife, a man may dream of past partners if they were more vibrant, emotional, and passionate.

3.   **Character and Behavior.** A man may lose interest in his wife not only due to problems in their intimate life but also because of a tense atmosphere in the family.

- Conflict and scandals – constant reproaches, shouting, and insults reduce sexual desire.

- Emotional tension – even if the woman does not mind sex but behaves rudely or creates constant stress, this can dampen the man's desire for intimacy.

- Lack of respect – if the wife allows herself to be disrespectful with words or actions towards her husband, over time, he begins to feel unnecessary.

4.   **The Man is Afraid of His Wife.** Some women can be overly emotional and temperamental.

- Fear of a scandal – if a man knows that any word or action can trigger a stormy reaction, he starts avoiding conflicts, including in the intimate sphere.

- Dominant behavior from the wife – if the man feels overwhelmed, this can reduce his attraction to his wife, but it will not reduce his need for sex.

Beauty is an important aspect of a woman's attractiveness, but it is far from the only one. For a man to stay engaged in the relationship, it is important to:

- Maintain emotional closeness.

- Diversify your intimate life.

- Create a comfortable atmosphere in the family.

- Treat each other with respect.

Infidelity is not always related to a woman's appearance. More often, it is the result of dissatisfaction in the relationship that builds up over time.

7 MISTAKES THAT PREVENT WOMEN FROM FINDING HAPPINESS AND BUILDING HARMONIOUS RELATIONSHIPS

Many women make the same mistakes in relationships without even realizing it. These mistakes can lead to disappointment, feelings of dissatisfaction, and even the breakdown of the family. We can look at the main ones and discuss how to avoid them.

1.   **Dissolving into the man.** Love is a balance between what we give and what we receive. However, some women become so absorbed in their relationships that they forget about themselves.

- The woman gives herself completely to the man, forgetting about her own needs.

- Self-sacrifice becomes the norm, and personal interests take a back seat.

- The man starts to take her selflessness for granted, not making an effort in return.

What to do? Maintain a balance between caring for your partner and paying attention to yourself. Relationships should bring joy to both parties, not turn into one-sided giving.

2.   **The misconception that care is the key to love.** Many women believe that by surrounding their man with maximum care, they will ensure a strong relationship. They begin to behave like "mothers" towards their partner: washing, cleaning, cooking, fulfilling all his requests.

- This behavior can only attract weak, infantile men who are used to being cared for.

- Strong and confident men value partnership, not maternal care.

What to do? Build a relationship on equal terms, without turning into a "servant."

3.   **Avoiding conflicts and suppressing emotions.** Some women learn from childhood that it is better to endure than to argue. They silently suffer, not expressing dissatisfaction, suppressing resentments.

- Problems are not solved but accumulate, causing irritation and disappointment.

- The man may not even realize that something is wrong if the woman does not talk about it.

- Keeping quiet leads to passive aggression, sarcasm, and hidden dissatisfaction.

In my book *The Simple Formula for Communication,* the topic of conflicts is thoroughly explored in the chapter *Why Do Conflicts Make Us Stronger and Closer?*

What to do? Learn to speak openly about your feelings and needs, but without aggression. Conflicts are not a sign of weakness, but a way to find a solution.

4. **The desire to be the "perfect" partner in the relationship.** Some women strive to make the relationship perfect by completely focusing on their partner.

- They place the man at the center of their life, forgetting about themselves.

- They stop developing, neglecting their hobbies and social circle.

- The man feels that he has become her only support, which can cause pressure and irritation.

What to do? Maintain your individuality, continue to develop, and do not limit your life to just the relationship.

5. Submitting to the Man's Demands. Sometimes, a man tries to control a woman by imposing how she should behave. For example:

- He forbids her from going to the gym because people look at her there.

- He disapproves of her meetings with friends.

- He limits her hobbies.

The woman starts sacrificing her interests for the sake of "peace in the family." Over time, this leads to the loss of her own individuality.

What to do? Stand up for your boundaries and interests. Healthy relationships are built on mutual respect, not strict control.

6. Expecting the Man to Guess Her Desires. Some women wait for the man to understand what is bothering them. They hope that he will "guess" their feelings, mood, and resentments.

- Men cannot read minds and often miss hidden signals.

- The woman feels offended but does not directly say what the problem is.

- The relationship turns into a guessing game, leading to misunderstandings and conflicts.

What to do? Talk about your needs openly, without hints or expecting the man to figure it out on his own.

7. Refusing to Acknowledge Weakness and Ask for Help. Some women believe they must be strong and handle everything on their own.

- They do not ask for support, even when they really need help.

- Over time, fatigue, disappointment, and the feeling that no one values their efforts accumulate.

- The relationship becomes unbalanced: The woman does everything herself, and the man becomes used to this.

What to do? Do not be afraid to ask for help and acknowledge your vulnerability. Healthy relationships are built on mutual support.

A woman's happiness is not about self-sacrifice, endurance, or perfect relationships "by the book." It is built on harmony between herself and the world around her.

To build strong and happy relationships, it is important to start with yourself. Love and respect yourself, openly share your feelings and desires, find balance between caring for your partner and attending to your own needs. Do not hesitate to ask for support and express your individuality. It is in such an atmosphere that true, harmonious relationships are born, where both feel good and at peace.

CONCLUSION

Male infidelity is not a coincidence, but the result of many factors: from unmet needs in the relationship to the man's inner insecurity. Often, infidelity occurs not because of a woman's appearance, but due to emotional coldness, a lack of intimacy, and accumulated resentments.

To protect your family from betrayal, it is important to learn how to talk about your feelings, work on trust, keep a lively interest in each other, and preserve the emotional connection. A woman's low self-esteem is one of the main "invisible" enemies of love. It affects her choice of partner, boundaries, and confidence. But the good news is that confidence can be developed.

Understanding the reasons for male infidelity, avoiding repeated female mistakes, and working on yourself — this is the path to harmonious relationships and true happiness.

CHAPTER 2.

REACTIONS AND STRATEGIES FOR DEALING WITH INFIDELITY

Infidelity is a blow that always catches you off guard. The heart screams, the mind is silent, and the body feels almost paralyzed. In this chapter, we will explore how to cope with shock, pain, feelings of rejection, and fear. You will learn how to behave in the first days after betrayal, what mistakes to avoid, and what steps truly help in recovery. If you have decided to save the family, we will discuss whether you can trust a man's promises, how much time he needs to forget the mistress, and how to deal with the anxiety that it might happen again. This chapter is not about weakness, but about strength: the strength to survive, understand, and choose your own path.

HOW TO COPE WITH THE PAIN OF A MAN'S BETRAYAL

Infidelity is one of the most painful events in life. If you have faced betrayal and feel like your world has collapsed, if it seems like a close person has betrayed you and you feel hurt, upset, angry, or humiliated, but you do not know how to ease your emotional state—let us work through this together.

Infidelity is not just about the betrayal of another person but also about the destruction of your own illusions. It is similar to a breakup. You lose not only the person but also what you believed in. Therefore, like any grief, you go through certain stages:

- Denial
- Anger and aggression
- Bargaining and guilt
- Depression and despair
- Acceptance

Acceptance is not necessarily about forgiveness and returning to the partner. It is an internal point where you simply acknowledge the fact of the infidelity and allow yourself to let go of the situation.

Emotions during this period can vary greatly: anger, rage, resentment, shame, humiliation—all of this is normal. It is important not to suppress emotions but express them in healthy ways—without harming yourself or others.

Infidelity always causes pain. For any woman, it is perceived as a betrayal of agreements, as a challenge: Why did he choose someone else and not me? There is a sense of competition, resentment, and humiliation. This is absolutely normal—such a situation triggers a storm of emotions.

Step 1. Acknowledge the Extent of Your Pain. Ask yourself: Is my pain a reaction to the infidelity itself, or is it much deeper? If you feel like you cannot escape the loop of thoughts, that the same moments keep playing over and over in your head, and the feelings do not subside—it is possible that you are facing pain that goes beyond the situation itself. This means the emotions are stuck, like a splinter, and you need to work through them.

Step 2. Live Through This Feeling. Do not avoid the pain — try to be with it. Recall the most painful moment: the message, the conversation, the fact. Allow yourself to feel and observe, without running away. Just be with that feeling as if you are standing by a loved one in trouble.

It is important to distinguish between empathy and compassion. You do not need to "fix" yourself, you need to be with yourself. Tell yourself, "I am sorry this happened. This hurts. I am with you." Embrace yourself.

Step 3. Give Your Emotions Form. Name what you are feeling. Is it anger towards your husband? Hatred for the mistress? Disappointment from unmet expectations? Or sadness from the loss of connection? Most likely, it is a tangle of emotions. Unwind it, give each emotion a name.

Step 4. Write Everything Down. If it is difficult to be alone with your feelings, use paper. Make it a rule to write down everything that comes to mind for 10 minutes a day. Do not filter, do not analyze — just let the thoughts flow. This is a way to give your inner world an outlet and reduce internal tension.

Step 5. Talk to a Close Person. If you have a friend, close friend, or parent you can trust — share with them. But do not burden your children with your emotions — they should not become your "therapists."

Step 6. Talk to a Psychologist. This is one of the safest and most effective ways to go through the pain consciously and with support.

Step 7. Talk to Your Partner. If possible, calmly discuss why this happened, what he feels, and share your own feelings. But do not delve into the details — that can only intensify the pain. The most important thing is to understand the reason and take a pause.

If you want to see yourself in a relationship built on love, mutual respect, trust, and the values most important to you, the first skill you need to master is healthy communication. To express your unmet needs without triggering defensiveness, resentment, or conflict from your partner, read my book, *The Simple Formula for Communication.*

Why Is This So Painful?

Sometimes infidelity becomes so destructive because it touches on old wounds — rejection, loneliness, neglect. If, in childhood, you experienced a lack of attention or emotional emptiness, infidelity may trigger the same feelings as back then.

But now you are not a child. You are an adult with resources, support, and the ability to cope. Remind yourself of this.

If you live together, it is not necessary to separate. Just let him know that you need time and space. Honestly say, "I need a couple of weeks of silence and peace to figure things out."

Do not rush to make a decision. You do not need to decide today or tomorrow: forgive or separate. Remember Scarlett O'Hara's phrase: "I will think about it tomorrow." Take your time. Stay in silence. Take care of yourself as you would care for a beloved child.

Take a hot bath, treat yourself to something delicious, buy yourself something nice, wrap yourself in a blanket. Allow yourself to feel, experience, and take care of yourself.

And most importantly, let time do its work. If you allow yourself to go through all the stages consciously, you will definitely feel how the pain subsides. Clarity will come, and the decision to stay or leave will arise on its own. And whatever you choose, it will already be your mature choice, not a decision made in the heat of pain.

You will cope. Just give yourself some time and love.

CAUGHT YOUR HUSBAND CHEATING, WHAT TO DO? 4 ACTIONS WHEN IN A STATE OF SHOCK

When you find out that your close partner has cheated on you, it becomes a real emotional explosion. The news literally crashes down, leaving you without support. In such moments, a person feels helpless, unable to help themselves, and unable to make a rational decision. It is unclear how to react to what is happening, how to behave with your partner. Everything becomes mixed up, and you lose your stability.

People who have experienced infidelity say that at the moment when everything is revealed, it is like they lose their head — it is as if reason has been cut off. While everything is calm, you can understand what happens in other relationships. But when it concerns you personally, rationality switches off.

The first thing you need to do is pay attention to your body. This will help you regain control over yourself and calm down.

1.   **Take control of yourself.** Literally touch and massage your head with your hands. Feel your face, skull, and consciously notice your body with your palms. This helps you concentrate, ground yourself, and return to reality.

2.   **Wash your face with cold water.** Cold water acts on the receptors and refreshes perception. Washing symbolizes the beginning of a new page. It helps you switch and gives you a sense of "here and now."

3.   **Hug yourself.** Exercise: Place your left hand under your right armpit, and with your right hand, hug yourself over your

left shoulder. This self-hug gives you a sense of security, as if someone is embracing you. This is especially important because infidelity always brings feelings of rejection, and it is crucial to feel that you are not alone.

4.   **Massage the area of your solar plexus (where the sternum and ribs meet).** This helps relieve tension in your body, shift attention from the internal "knot," and remove the feeling of a taut string, which often arises in moments of intense stress.

Rational attempts to calm yourself in such moments do not work. But body practices do help because you cannot deceive your body. By performing these simple actions, you can feel support, even if only for a few minutes. This is the first step toward recovery.

Infidelity always destroys the script of the future. A close person, who was part of your plans, suddenly disappears from them, and the future seems blurry, dark, and frightening. In such a situation, any productive activity will help cope with anxiety. This can be cleaning, sorting through your wardrobe, planning upcoming goals, or cooking. Any familiar activity that does not require learning helps calm down and regain control over the situation.

It is impossible to radically change plans for the future. However, you can write tactical plans at least for a few days: what to do today, tomorrow, and by the end of the week. This will create a sense of stability and confidence in the days ahead.

It Is Very Important to Speak Out. When a person finds out about infidelity, a huge amount of emotions builds up inside them, and they want to spill these feelings onto the betrayer.

However, such conversations are rarely constructive, especially if the person is in strong emotional turmoil. It is important to find a safe way to express your feelings: talk to a close person, a therapist, or even just write about your emotions in a journal. By describing your emotions on paper, you can see the situation from a different perspective and partially let go of the pain.

Over time, the trauma of infidelity will begin to subside. Tomorrow might feel easier, in a week it will be a little simpler, and in a month — even more. However, the process of healing is often uneven: There may be days when the pain resurfaces. It is important to remember that, over time, it will still weaken.

If it is hard to cope on your own, you can turn to a specialist who will help you process your emotions more quickly and effectively. The key is to start with yourself and try to calm down.

HOW TO SURVIVE THE FIRST DAYS AFTER INFIDELITY: IMPORTANT RULES AND MISTAKES TO AVOID

What to do in the first days after infidelity?

Step 1. Allow yourself to experience your emotions. You are experiencing a storm of feelings: sadness, rage, fear, confusion, resentment. Do not try to hold back these emotions. Allow yourself to cry or scream, give yourself time for the wave of emotions to subside.

Step 2. Find support. Call a friend, a close friend, or your mother (if she is supportive and not critical). Think about who you can talk to and share what happened. By telling the situation over and over, you will help yourself deal with the trauma.

Step 3. See a specialist. A psychologist or therapist can help you understand what has happened and guide you in the right direction.

Step 4. Talk to your husband. This step is difficult, but necessary. If you have evidence (messages, receipts, payments for flowers and gifts you did not receive), show them. If you only have suspicions, think carefully about whether to start the conversation. Be prepared for him to deny the affair. The main thing is to stay calm, talk about your feelings, and ask for honesty.

Step 5. Give yourself time to make a decision. You need time to sort through your emotions and decide what to do next. If you have children and do not want to disrupt their routine, ask him to stay in another room. If being together is unbearable, he should leave. This is not a decision to make hastily. It will determine your future life, happiness, and emotional and mental well-being.

What should you NOT do?

- Isolate yourself, avoid support.

- Think that you are unimportant to anyone.

- Ignore the problem, hoping it will resolve itself.

- Immediately go on a trip together to "turn the page."

- Publicly confront the mistress.

- Cheat on your husband in revenge.

- Immediately file for divorce without carefully considering everything.

- Share the details of the betrayal with your children.

It is important to decide whether you need this person in your life. If you do, it is one standard of behavior. If you do not, it is a completely different one. You cannot push the gas and brake at the same time, like in a car. This leads to confusion and worsens the situation. A woman may genuinely want to keep her husband: because of love, children, financial dependence, fear of being alone, or insecurity. But her actions — reproaches, insults, emotional outbursts — contradict her goal of saving the relationship. In the end, he leaves, even though she would have wanted him to stay.

When you find out about infidelity, the first thing is to honestly formulate your attitude: Do you want to save the marriage or not? Then, seek support from a professional: a psychologist or a psychotherapist. Do not take suspicions as facts. Find real evidence of infidelity: take photos of the conversation, find receipts for flowers and gifts. In reality, the man may not be cheating but simply spending time with friends or colleagues, and even geolocation does not give the full picture.

Therefore, if infidelity has occurred — sit down and think about whether you want your husband. If you do, seek help, and get the opinion of an authoritative specialist. Then, create a list of demands for your husband: for example, end the relationship with the other woman, change jobs, be open in communication, come home on time, spend time with the family. Without a clear course of action, it will be difficult to regain trust.

You also need to be honest with yourself and set demands for yourself. This does not mean you are at fault. But in some cases, there are indeed gaps in the relationship that are worth paying attention to. This could be a lack of intimacy, indifference, changes in appearance, or a change in how you see yourself. This is not a reason for guilt, but an opportunity for growth.

So, the decision about your husband, clear demands from him, and clear demands from yourself. If all of this is in place, you will be able to move forward and not get stuck in pain. The hardest part about infidelity is not the infidelity itself, but the fact that people do not know what to do next. In such a situation, the husband is unlikely to guide you on the right path. Therefore, after experiencing the initial emotions, it is important to keep a cool head, so that, without giving in to emotions, you can create a plan of action. Only a firm position and specific actions will help you direct the situation in the right direction. And most importantly, understand where exactly you want to end up.

TWO MORE WAYS TO COPE WITH THE PAIN OF REJECTION

What to do to cope with the pain of rejection? Infidelity is a serious psychological trauma. Often, a person experiences contradictory feelings: "I cannot live without him," "Go away," "Stay," "Let us start over." These "emotional swings" can last a long time.

Here are two exercises that can help:

Exercise 1. Feel like an adult. Touch yourself and say aloud: "I, [your name], I am [your age] years old. I control my life. I know how to take care of myself. I have already grown up. Infidelity is painful, but it does not threaten my life." This exercise helps you step out of the childlike position and see the situation through adult eyes.

Exercise 2. Stand in front of the mirror and say: "I am an adult person. I am the most important and chosen person for myself. I value my life, my uniqueness, and my self-worth." This will help you regain a sense of inner support and value, reducing the sharpness of the emotional experience.

These exercises should be repeated until the pain subsides. Sometimes, only a specialist can help you understand the deep reactions to betrayal. After all, the pain of rejection goes back to our childhood and has a huge influence on the life of an adult.

The pain of betrayal can be unbearable. When you find out that your spouse is cheating, it may feel like something is dying inside, and the question arises: What should I do next?

Sometimes divorce seems like the only way out, but in some cases, it can be difficult to decide if it is really the best solution.

Infidelity is a betrayal by a spouse or partner, which can include both physical and emotional deception. Emotional infidelity can be expressed in a deep attachment to another person, sharing personal experiences with them, or participating in online relationships. Physical infidelity involves intimacy. Both types of infidelity can destroy a relationship, making the partner feel unwanted and rejected.

When should you leave after infidelity? There is no universal answer — each situation is individual. If the infidelity was a one-time mistake, the partner sincerely regrets it and is ready to work on the relationship, there is a chance to save it. However, this will require a lot of effort and time.

If the partner does not regret his actions, does not take responsibility, continues to cheat, or does not want to work on rebuilding trust, these are warning signs. In this case, you should consider whether you can trust him again. If the answer is "no," it may be better to end the relationship.

It is important to consider your well-being. If the pain is too intense and it seems impossible to get over the infidelity, divorce may be the best option. If you are unsure about your decision, it is worth consulting a psychologist who can help you understand your feelings and possible options.

If you have decided to stay in the relationship, it is necessary to take steps toward healing. A conversation with your partner will help you understand why this happened and how to avoid similar situations in the future. It is important to develop a plan for further action, and possibly consult a family counselor.

Forgiveness is necessary to move forward, but it does not mean forgetting the betrayal. It is the realization of what happened and the decision not to dwell on the pain. Rebuilding trust is the most difficult stage, requiring patience and effort. However, if both partners are willing to work on it, over time, the pain can be overcome, and strong, loyal relationships can be built.

When you have done everything possible, but the relationship still has not been restored, it is not your fault. Perhaps it is time to acknowledge that a marriage depends on both partners, and if one is not ready to preserve it, letting go might be the best decision.

The topic of forgiveness of betrayal is explored in more detail in the book *How to Deal with a Love Triangle.*

YOU HAVE DECIDED TO SAVE THE FAMILY—HOW MUCH TIME DOES A MAN NEED TO FORGET HIS MISTRESS?

To be honest, for a man who had a serious, emotionally intense, and long-term relationship with his mistress—say, several years—it may be impossible to completely forget her. But this is not a cause for panic. We all remember the vivid moments of our lives, including school years or childhood arguments. These memories remain, but they no longer control our lives or influence our behavior.

The same goes for memories of the mistress—even if a man remembers, it does not mean he is still emotionally involved. He can continue living on.

If the relationship was brief, not very passionate, the memories may fade within a few months. Sometimes, men do not even remember the woman's name—the connection was so insignificant.

However, in the "classic" case, when the relationship lasted about a year, the breakup leaves an emotional mark for roughly the same period. The most intense period is the first three months. This is related to hormonal attachment and biological mechanisms: After intimacy, the man's brain, like the woman's, assumes the possibility of conception, and this triggers long-term emotional involvement.

To ease the process of "forgetting," a man should:

- Cut off all communication with the former mistress.
- Get rid of things associated with her.

51

- Stop following her on social media.

- Actively focus on recovery: pay attention to intimacy with his wife, engage in interesting activities, work, and new projects.

Emotional richness in life is very helpful. If, after the breakup, the man experiences vivid emotions within the family or gets inspired by work or hobbies — this is the best way to return to normal more quickly.

If, however, life becomes empty, there is a high chance that one mistress will be replaced by another — just to fill the emotional void. That is why it is important to create an environment in the family or in your life that has support, warmth, interest, joy, and drive.

Some men fall into depression, and in that case, professional help is necessary. But in most cases, with an active and vibrant life, a person can fully recover in 3 to 12 months.

It is important to understand even if a man remembers the mistress, it does not mean he cannot be happy in his family. The key is to return to goals and interests, making the marriage rich and valuable.

A Man's Life Is Not Just About Relationships — It Is Career, Hobbies, Creativity, and Self-Realization. It is not worth spending years on regrets. You need to move forward and build a new, full, and interesting life.

What to Do If a Husband Cannot Forget His Mistress?

When a man ends his relationship with a mistress, especially under pressure from his wife, but cannot forget her, it becomes a serious trial for the whole family. Women in this situation suffer greatly: They see that something is wrong with their husband. He becomes lost, gloomy, depressed, sometimes aggressive, or on the contrary, withdrawn and distant.

The wife may feel: "If you are so miserable without her — go to her! Why torture both yourself and me?" She is overwhelmed with emotions. Sometimes, unable to bear it, she creates major arguments, eventually kicking her husband out or bringing the situation to the point where he leaves on his own. And unfortunately, in this situation, the mistress wins: She gets the man "on a silver platter."

The transition from the mistress to the family is smoother and more active if the man moves out, or if the mistress moves to another city, or if the wife begins working with her husband, sharing interesting activities and common goals.

But if nothing in the man's life has changed — the same job, the same routine, everything is as before, just without the mistress — then he may sink into depression. The acute period of suffering can last three months, and complete recovery may take up to a year.

What should the wife do? The key is to be patient. Avoid provoking unnecessary conflicts, but do not let the man retreat into himself without an outlet. If he suddenly talks about his feelings, listen. Yes, it is hard. But it is better to give him an emotional outlet than to let him reach an internal breakdown.

And one more thing: Do not impose yourself. At such moments, it is important not to pressure him, not to demand attention, and not to try to "replace" the mistress with excessive care. Patience and tactful presence are your best allies in this difficult process.

As painful as it may sound, if a man has fallen in love with the mistress, experienced spectacular sex, vivid emotions, and romance with her, and then returned to the family after 5, 10, or even 20 years of marriage, do not expect him to immediately adjust. Some men truly try to return to the family and genuinely make an effort, but if family life lacks vivid emotions, this process will be very difficult. Achieving emotional fulfillment after many years of living together can be challenging.

So, dear wives, if you see that your husband is struggling, feeling down, or gloomy, try to spend as little time as possible with him at home. Look for new places: walk through new streets, go to new cafes, promenades, or shopping centers. Book trips, even for the weekend — let them be inexpensive hotels or short trips to nearby cities. The key is a change of scenery, new experiences, novelty. This will create a sense of a new life, a new page, and help the man shift his focus.

Home is the place where memories, thoughts, and comparisons live. So, try to get your husband out of the house, not letting him dwell on it. If you cannot go away, invite friends, arrange gatherings, and socializing. It is important that there is life, movement, and conversation in the house — not isolation and silence.

In addition to this, do not forget about intimacy and kindness. This helps restore the connection and remind you both why you are together. A man who is trying to forget his mistress is experiencing internal dependence. His brain is still holding onto memories and a sense of responsibility for that woman. Often, a relationship with a mistress forms an illusion: "I am needed by her, she cannot manage without me." Therefore, a man needs time for his brain to realize she is living her life, everything is fine with her, and his care is no longer needed.

At the same time, his brain may start looking for an excuse to argue with you. He will latch onto small things to convince himself: "I am not happy here, I am not understood. I need to go back to where real love was." Do not fall for the provocation. If you get irritated, criticize, or argue — it will only push him toward leaving. And then, sadly, you will be the one giving the mistress a gift.

Yes, it may be hard — your husband is lying on the couch, does not want to do anything, and behaves distantly. But this needs to be endured. Do not let conflicts become an excuse for him to leave. Even if he slams the door and says, "I cannot do this anymore," let it be his decision and his responsibility. Calmness and tact are your allies.

Remember: Over the years of living together, you have already told all the jokes and discussed all the topics. He may be bored not because you are bad, but because everything has long been familiar. New people, new emotions, new topics of conversation — these are what help revive everyday life.

Intimacy is also important, but it does not always happen right away. It is a process. What matters now is patience, living communication, movement, new experiences, and the absence of pressure.

And most importantly — do not rush to "give" your husband to the mistress. Believe me, she may be waiting for the moment when he breaks from the internal tension and returns to her. Do not give her that joy. You still have every chance to restore the relationship and begin a new stage — a more conscious, mature, and lively one.

SHOULD YOU BELIEVE YOUR HUSBAND WHEN HE PROMISES TO BREAK UP WITH HIS MISTRESS?

When a man says, "I have made up my mind, I am breaking up with the mistress," it may sound reassuring to his wife. Especially if she sincerely hopes that he will really cut all contacts. But, unfortunately, in practice, it is not that simple.

If it was a fleeting affair, with rare meetings and no strong emotional attachment—then yes, a man can really end the relationship quickly. But if the affair lasted more than six months, especially several years, simply saying "I have made up my mind" is not enough. In most cases, it is just words.

Breaking up with a mistress, especially if the woman is still reaching out, waiting for him, reminding him of herself, and is not categorically ending the relationship, rarely happens without a trace. If the mistress invested emotions, hopes, years of her life, dreamed of having a child or a family with him—she will not just disappear. She will send signals, evoke regret, and pull him back.

It is very difficult for a man in this situation to completely sever the connection. Even if he says everything is over, a few days or weeks later, he may experience a strong psychological and even physical withdrawal. Insomnia sets in, appetite disappears, anxiety rises, and all he can think is "How is she? What is happening with her?" This is the so-called "withdrawal syndrome"—the body and mind demand to return to the usual emotional state.

It is especially hard if the man had regular, passionate intimate relations with the mistress. A man's brain, by nature, perceives this as a possible pregnancy and activates the "protect, care, be close" program. This is why the man may literally be torn between his feelings for his wife and his attachment to the mistress.

It is also important to understand: A man often cannot determine his priorities by himself. Today he may consider his wife the most important, but tomorrow he may feel drawn to the mistress. These emotional swings are caused by hormonal fluctuations, and at this moment, it is truly difficult for the man. He is torn, confused, and experiences feelings of guilt, irritation, sadness — all at once.

What Should the Wife Do?

First of all, do not relax after hearing, "I have made up my mind." Even if you really want to believe that it is all over, most often, the attempts to reconnect with the mistress will still happen. Your task is not to nag, not to start arguments, not to pressure him. On the contrary, you need to be there, create emotional warmth, interest, and closeness. Support your husband, be his confidante, lover, and friend.

But at the same time be vigilant. Carefully and unobtrusively observe: Is communication being resumed? Are there any messages, calls, meetings? Without excessive control, but with reasonable attention. Because in the months following the breakup, a man may still have an obsessive desire to restore things.

It is important not to start fights. A man, experiencing an internal conflict, may unconsciously provoke you into arguments to "justify" his return to the mistress. He will tell himself: "See, things are not working with my wife, she does not understand me, I am going to the one who understands me." Do not give him that reason.

Stay calm. Support him, but do not lose yourself in him completely. Do not lose your sense of self, maintain your dignity. Remember: A wife's emotional stability is the anchor that helps her husband weather the storm.

And finally, the most important thing: If you want to save the family, you will have to invest in rebuilding the relationship. Create a new, deeper connection. Because if nothing changes in the family, if everything goes back to the way it was, the man may start looking for those emotions and feelings again — outside the family.

Yes, the process of recovery may not take weeks, but months; sometimes up to a year. But with the right approach, patience, and reasonable involvement, it can end with the man truly staying with you — consciously, with an understanding of the value of your relationship.

FEAR THAT THE MAN WILL CHEAT AND LEAVE

Many women experience the fear: "What if my man cheats and leaves?" This fear is familiar to most, and it is completely normal. After all, men sometimes cheat, families break up, and divorce statistics confirm this. Such topics are often discussed in the media, online, and on social networks. Gradually, this fear can grow into an obsessive state, a female phobia, a neurosis that interferes with building harmonious relationships.

But it is important to understand a few things.

First, it is not just men who cheat, but women as well. Moreover, the number of women cheating in marriage is also increasing. Social media, dating sites, and active communication at work contribute to this. So, the fear of being betrayed is not just a woman's fear. Men also fear losing their woman — fear infidelity. This is a common human fear, and it can become a reason to strengthen relationships, not destroy them.

Second, men do not leave just like that. Almost always, before leaving, they send signals. They say: "Please, be kinder," "Let us spend more time together," "Talk to me, not your phone," "Let us do something together," "Pay attention to your appearance, intimacy, and household." They ask not in an ultimatum, but as partners who want to improve the relationship. A woman who is afraid of losing her man can always hear these signals and take steps to get closer. This does not mean the man is bad. He just has needs — the same as the woman.

Third, fear, in itself, is useless. Being afraid that something will happen does not protect you from it. We all know that we will die one day—but that does not stop us from making plans, working, living, and loving. It is the same here: Fearing that the man will leave does not mean preventing it. It is much more important to understand how male psychology works, what his needs are, and what is important to him in a relationship. Then, you will not just "fear," but will act from a position of strength, understanding, and maturity.

Men need to feel significant, supported, and believed in. And when a woman does not play the role of a victim but becomes a true partner—confident, kind, interesting, inspiring—the man does not leave. He feels good by her side and appreciates such a woman.

It is important to understand, dear women, you have the "remote control" for your relationships. You can steer them in the right direction, creating the atmosphere that makes him want to stay. Do not trap yourself in fears, do not think that all men are just waiting for a chance to leave. That is not true. Most men want to be with their loved one, with children, with their family. They just need to feel needed, appreciated, and believed in.

HOW TO OVERCOME THE FEAR OF INFIDELITY: A STEP-BY-STEP GUIDE TO INNER CALM

Imagine: you have a relationship with a man, everything seems perfect, but the thought keeps running through your mind — what if he is cheating? You start checking his phone, looking through his social media, monitoring his likes, digging through his browser history. The more you search and find nothing, the more convinced you become — he is just hiding the evidence well. You need to dig deeper.

As a result, you spoil your own mood, lose your emotional balance, and stop enjoying the relationship. Moreover, you start destroying the relationship by poisoning it with suspicions and anxiety.

The fear of infidelity often arises without objective reasons and turns into an obsessive state. This is bad because it triggers the "self-fulfilling prophecy" effect: If you constantly suspect your partner, accuse him, become jealous, and question him about colleagues, you create a sense of guilt for things he has not done. He starts feeling that infidelity is a possible scenario and becomes more receptive to attention from other women. And then — infidelity may actually happen.

It is important to understand: If a man cheats, he is fully responsible for it. But if a woman's behavior constantly creates tension and violates boundaries, she also participates in the destruction of the relationship. You cannot constantly suspect and still hope for trust and harmony.

Where does the fear of infidelity come from in the first place? Historically, ideal relationships were perceived as a lifelong union—"until death do us part." Society supported these relationships: small villages, the church, morals, the impossibility of divorce. People lived with their partners for life, even if feelings faded.

Today, things are different. We live longer, have access to an endless number of new acquaintances, move around, travel. There are more relationships, but there are no skills to properly end them. Often, when relationships have run their course, people continue living together, ignoring reality. The woman goes into motherhood or domestic life, and the man finds someone else on the side.

And so, infidelity becomes a way to exit a relationship without directly saying it is over.

Therefore, overcoming the fear of infidelity means understanding its nature, learning to have honest dialogue, and recognizing the crisis in time so that it can be addressed, rather than hiding from it in anxiety or suspicion. It is important to trust, develop emotional closeness, and be able to calmly end a relationship if it has truly come to an end.

How to Overcome the Fear of Infidelity?

Sometimes a man cheats on a woman. If she finds out but pretends nothing happened—represses, ignores, or suppresses her emotions—the relationship becomes formal. They live together, but in essence, they are already apart. The man continues to cheat, and the woman pretends not to notice.

But if this is unacceptable to the woman and she leaves, she often removes the man's responsibility for the breakup. He can say, "She left on her own. I was not planning to end the relationship." Therefore, the fear of infidelity is often actually the fear of the relationship ending. The fear that the person will not gather the courage to talk honestly and will simply leave, betraying.

For women, the fear of infidelity is most often connected to two reasons:

1.   **Personal experience.** If a relationship ended due to infidelity in the past, especially if it was sudden and painful, the woman may unconsciously expect this scenario to repeat. When we are cheated on, we experience double pain: on one side — sadness from the loss, on the other — anger and frustration from betrayal. These emotions intertwine, and as a result, we cannot "properly" let go of the person. The relationship remains unfinished, and in a new union, the woman lives in expectation that everything will repeat itself.

2.   **Low self-esteem.** A woman may feel she is "not good enough." And if she does not value herself, it is logical to assume that the man will not value her either, and sooner or later, he will reject her. One of the most frightening scenarios is infidelity.

What to do if you fear infidelity?

Here are three important steps:

Step 1: Work on your self-esteem. Start doing things that make you feel proud. Learn new skills, try hobbies, expand your social circle. This could be learning a foreign language, driving a car, dancing, participating in new projects. Your self-esteem strengthens when you begin to value yourself and gain recognition from others. Then you move out of the "I'm not good enough" position and become confident in your worth.

Step 2: Paradoxical intention. If the obsessive thought that your partner is cheating on you tortures you, try this exercise. Take a piece of paper and describe the worst-case scenario: "The man cheats on me with my best friend, everyone finds out, we get divorced, and I do not know what to do next." Write it in detail, with maximum catastrophe. When you face this fear head-on, it will lose some of its power. Realizing that even in the worst case, you will manage, you will feel more confident.

Step 3: Establish emotional contact. If you cannot directly talk about the fear of infidelity, start with small steps — share your emotions. Say things like, "I feel sad," "I am anxious," "I feel lonely." Learn to listen to your partner and create an atmosphere of openness. Over time, you will have the opportunity to discuss deeper fears. When there is trust between you, your partner can genuinely reassure you.

But if the anxiety is too strong, you cannot manage jealousy, and your mind suggests that there is no real reason to worry, then it might be worth seeking help from a psychotherapist. Sometimes the reasons are deeper than they seem, and an individual approach will help the most.

Relationships are about trust. And trust begins with self-confidence and the ability to talk about your feelings. Take care of yourself, preserve your emotional balance, and create relationships where there is honesty, support, and love.

Surviving infidelity means going through a storm of emotions, finding support within yourself, and making a conscious decision to stay or leave. Reactions may vary, but it is important not to lose yourself in this pain. A well-thought-out strategy is not about revenge, but about caring for yourself and your boundaries. You have the right to anger, tears, silence, and a pause. The most important thing is to remember that even after infidelity, you can build a new version of yourself and your life, where there is room for respect, love, and peace.

WHEN THE HEART IS ON FIRE: WHERE JEALOUSY COMES FROM AND HOW TO DEAL WITH IT

Let us now talk about a very painful topic—jealousy. At some point, all of us encounter this feeling. Many people wonder whether jealousy is an essential part of love.

From an evolutionary perspective, jealousy is indeed a product of natural selection. People began to experience jealousy in ancient times when they transitioned from chaotic sexual relationships to monogamous unions, when stable couples started forming. This shift was a consequence of human progress. As men developed tools and learned to accumulate material wealth, new questions arose for women: "After his death, who (which woman) will inherit what he has accumulated?"

Surprisingly, economic relationships are closely intertwined with biological ones. This mechanism led to the formation of more stable unions—monogamous relationships. Yet, concerns about a partner's true faithfulness continued to arise.

For men, jealousy has always been a serious issue. Why? Because, to some extent, a man may question whether he is raising his own child. Unlike a woman, who is always certain she is the biological mother, a man has no such certainty. This is precisely why, in many cases, newborn babies tend to resemble their fathers more than their mothers—nature's way of ensuring that the father, upon looking at his child, instinctively recognizes him as his own.

For men, sexual infidelity is more traumatic, which is why their jealousy is strongly focused on the sexual aspect. For women, it is somewhat different. Since ancient times, women have understood the importance of emotional attachment from a man. Emotional commitment to a specific woman largely ensures that, despite various temptations, he will continue to care for her offspring. This is why women find it much harder to cope when a man falls in love with another woman, while viewing sexual infidelity more leniently.

What is Jealousy?

Jealousy is, in many ways, similar to neurosis. A person becomes fixated, loses the ability to function normally, struggles with sleep, and finds it difficult to think clearly. It resembles anxiety, which is why dealing with retrospective jealousy follows the same principles as managing neurosis. The key is continuous self-analysis — understanding what is happening within oneself, assessing how real the perceived threat is, and whether it truly endangers the relationship. People often keep journals, write down their thoughts, and analyze them later. Classic tools from cognitive-behavioral therapy can be helpful.

At its core, jealousy is a feeling of anxiety and distress — a fear that the person we love might be taken from us. There is a perceived threat to the relationship, a belief that someone else could take our place. This is one form of jealousy.

In reality, jealousy is not always directed at someone; it can also be directed at something. For example, people may feel jealous of the time their partner spends elsewhere, like with friends. Why does a wife feel intense jealousy when her husband plays football? Or why does a husband become frustrated when his wife goes out with her friends? He might perceive it as indifference towards him because her time and attention are being directed elsewhere.

Jealousy is closely linked to a fundamental way we interact with the world—control. The more jealous a person is, the stronger their desire to establish control over the object of their attachment. I deliberately avoid using the word "love" because love and fidelity are not necessarily tied to infidelity. If you look deeper, jealousy, and this is my personal opinion, is actually about our own relationship with ourselves.

Jealousy is a feeling rooted in how we interact with our self-perception. If I deeply believe that I am not "good enough," that I lack the qualities necessary to be successful with women or in social life, I will also struggle to believe that anything good can truly happen to me. Even when I receive signals of love, I will not trust them. More than that, I will constantly be scanning my surroundings for threats. I will check my partner's phone, peek into their emails, and call them three times an hour.

Because deep down, my inner belief tells me: "No, no, they cannot truly love you. No, no, this is not real." And since we all live within the limits of our own beliefs, we unconsciously trap ourselves within them. We dig and dig until we finally find *something,* even the smallest evidence. And once we do, we create complications and make the relationship unbearable.

Jealousy can also have a slightly different nature. In reality, low self-esteem is the central factor. The worse I feel about myself, the more I will experience jealousy toward my partner. For example, if I have insecurities in areas that are important to me and someone else appears who excels in those areas, I will feel jealous of that person because I perceive them as superior.

For instance, men who have insecurities about their sexual abilities will often, upon seeing another man, immediately worry that he may be better at satisfying women. If a man has a height complex, he will feel jealous of taller men. If he has insecurities about financial stability, he will be more jealous of men who can effortlessly pay the bill at the most expensive restaurants. In other words, jealousy is directed toward the area where I feel vulnerable and see another person excelling.

Jealousy can also stem from possessiveness. Tyrants — people who are used to completely consuming their partner — may themselves be unfaithful. And often, they do it consciously. These individuals are the first to accuse their partner, suspecting them of the same actions they are guilty of. This is known as projection — attributing our own internal motives to another person.

The logic goes: "If I cheat, if I stray, then my partner must be doing the same." This projection serves as a way to reduce guilt over their own infidelity. Such a person will eagerly look for reasons to be jealous, using accusations as a means to reconcile with their guilty conscience.

Jealousy is an emotion that drains energy. It is also a feeling that often reinforces family conditioning. For example, if a girl grows up in a family where her mother constantly says, "Men cannot be trusted," or a boy hears from his father, "All women cheat, all women are unfaithful," then that child internalizes this belief.

Even if they later meet a completely loyal, kind, and trustworthy partner, they will still carry a deep, fundamental conviction: "No one can be trusted, I will be deceived, all women cheat, men cannot be trusted." As a result, they will look for endless reasons to feel jealous and start conflicts.

What is most interesting is that after repeated accusations and jealous outbursts, the partner may begin to internalize those same beliefs. They might start thinking, "Maybe I really am not enough... Maybe she is jealous because she is insecure..." The jealous person unconsciously creates a self-fulfilling prophecy, pulling their relationship back into the same toxic dynamic they absorbed from their upbringing, just to confirm their old beliefs.

That is why I strongly recommend breaking free from limiting beliefs. Stepping outside of them is not easy, but remember this: If at some point you decided that "all people cheat," that was your personal choice. And if you continue down the road of relationships while projecting this belief onto every person you meet, planting it in their subconscious like a hypnotic suggestion, then inevitably, that is exactly what you will experience in return.

I always recommend working on self-esteem if you feel jealous even when:

- Your partner does not give you any real reasons to doubt them.

- They do not hide their phone password.

- They do not take their phone to the bathroom.

- They do not get drunk at parties and act inappropriately with guests.

Ask yourself: "Do I need to focus more on my self-esteem? Should I build my confidence? Can I find inner stability so that I stop comparing myself to others?"

Jealousy always stems from endless comparisons. Shift your focus away from your partner. Perhaps you are idealizing them or attributing all possible virtues to them. Stop your fixation on them and redirect your energy toward yourself and your own growth. There is so much more to life than constantly monitoring and trying to control someone. People do not like being endlessly controlled; they feel psychological pressure and instinctively try to break free. And they do it in different ways.

That is why I highly recommend that whenever jealousy strikes, practice meditation, fill yourself with self-love, go to the gym. Never snoop through your partner's phone looking for something suspicious. Instead, find engaging hobbies, develop new skills, and focus on your own life.

Of course, self-esteem is key. A mature person with healthy self-worth understands that both partners are responsible for a relationship. You cannot fully control it one hundred percent of the time. You can love your partner, but you cannot suffocate them with your love. You can cherish them, but you cannot force them to be with you. You can appreciate them, but you should never devalue yourself in the process.

Choose yourself. Find the strength within to truly love and accept yourself. Loving yourself does not mean being self-absorbed; it means embracing who you are. Once you truly meet yourself, you will never lose yourself again. And then, jealousy will no longer be necessary.

CHAPTER 3

FORGIVE, LEAVE, OR ELIMINATE THE MISTRESS?

When a woman faces infidelity, she is faced with a painful choice: forgive, leave, or fight for the man by removing the rival. This chapter is not about sharp emotions but about deep analysis: can the relationship be restored, is it worth saving, and how to deal with the pain, betrayal, and love triangle.

Here, you will find an honest conversation about which infidelities can be forgiven and which should absolutely not be. You will learn how to survive betrayal, how to get your husband back (if that is what you really want) or how to let go and start a new life. We will also discuss the most difficult topic: how to "eliminate" the mistress without hysteria, but with dignity.

The most important thing is that you will not be left alone with the pain. This chapter will give you clarity, support, and a step-by-step plan on how to come out of the crisis stronger than before.

THE MOST EFFECTIVE WAY TO GET REVENGE ON A MAN FOR CHEATING

Many women, when faced with betrayal, experience a strong desire to get revenge. They want the man to regret his actions. Some even take a desperate step — they start an affair and tell their partner about it: "You cheated on me, so I will cheat on you." But in reality, such "revenge" only brings inner emptiness and disappointment.

Infidelity is usually not a spontaneous act. The reasons can be varied. And yes, sometimes a woman can, knowingly or unknowingly, contribute to the man straying. But that is not the focus here.

The question is: Should you seek revenge? And if so, how can you do it in a way that does not destroy yourself even more?

The most powerful way to "get revenge" on a man for infidelity is to become happy.

Yes, that is right. Do not throw tantrums, do not get revenge in kind, do not write tearful posts with autumn leaves and quotes about betrayal. Simply pull yourself together and start living for yourself.

This is not about pretending or forcing a smile. It is about real changes: in style, in mood, in life. Do something you have long dreamed of. Try a new hobby. Change something about yourself. Spend more time with friends, travel, grow. Not to prove something to someone. But for yourself.

When the man sees that you no longer suffer, that you are bright, confident, and free, that will be the strongest response to his actions. Because he will realize that he has lost something truly valuable. And you are not the one who stayed in the past, but the one who is moving forward.

But do not turn this goal into an obsession. Do not live just to make him regret it. Do it first and foremost for yourself.

Important: Do not engage in meaningless conversations, texts, or arguments with your ex. He may write, "Sorry, I did not think it would turn out this way," but do not give in. Ignoring him is the best tactic. Focus on yourself. Focus on your life.

Set specific goals for yourself: sports, a healthy lifestyle, new hobbies, creativity, spiritual development. Let interesting people, trips, and projects enter your life. This way, you will not only distract yourself but also feel the hormonal boost from positive changes. And most importantly—you will truly get to know yourself, this new, strong, real version of yourself.

Do not take revenge on the man with infidelity. If your relationship ended because of betrayal, simply erase him from your life and start living happily.

That is the "secret."

And if it is hard for you, if you cannot cope with your emotions, do not know how to restore your self-esteem, or how to live through this situation, do not be afraid to seek support. The most important thing is not to get stuck in the pain, but to move forward. Step by step. For yourself.

HOW TO FORGIVE INFIDELITY AND REBUILD THE FAMILY: STEPS TO FORGIVENESS AND HEALING

The topic of forgiving infidelity is discussed in more detail in the book *How to Deal with a Love Triangle*. This book covers all the nuances of forgiveness. I strongly recommend reading *How to Deal with a Love Triangle* to deeply understand all the elements of the process of forgiving betrayal.

In this chapter, we will look at forgiveness from the perspective of a situation where you have decided to save the relationship and the family.

Can a relationship be saved after infidelity? How can one cope with the pain of betrayal? This is one of the most difficult topics a couple can face. And each person has their own story.

Sometimes it is truly impossible to save the family; there are too many resentments, scandals, and aggression. But there are cases when a partner genuinely regrets their actions and wants to make things right. They understand how important you are to them. And despite the love, pain, disappointment, and inner emptiness get in your way.

What happens to a person after infidelity?

When we get married, we bring with us hopes, dreams, and sometimes even childhood traumas. We open up to our partner, expecting acceptance and love. And then ... betrayal. Everything we believed in crashes down. Old resentments and fears resurface: "I am not beautiful," "I am a failure," "I am not the way I should be." And the pain feels unbearable.

It is important to remember that this pain is temporary. Yes, it is intense, but it must be experienced. Do not hide behind work, do not pretend that "everything is fine." Suppressed emotions do not go away, and they can lead to illness and deep internal turmoil.

Cry. Scream. Talk about what you are feeling. Give yourself time. Do not be afraid to seem weak — there is no shame in that. Seek support from friends, family, or a therapist. Exercise, find a new hobby, travel — do everything that brings you back to life.

If your partner regrets their actions, it is important to recognize that. They are struggling too. If you decide to save the relationship, express your feelings — not with reproach, but with sincerity: "I am in pain," "I am struggling," "I cannot forget this." Give them the chance to be by your side through this process.

It will not all disappear immediately. It might take a year or two before you feel calm again. Do not blame yourself for that. Pain does not disappear with the snap of a finger. But if you have decided to save your family, act based on that decision.

Do not pretend everything is fine. Be honest in your sadness, but do not destroy it. Do not endlessly reproach — no one can handle that. Become a team. Face the crisis together.

Important: Do not make decisions in the heat of emotions. Imagine your life in five years. Where are you? Who are you with? What do you really want? Do you have children, a shared history, many years of life together? Think about whether it is worth destroying everything because of one mistake, even if it is a painful one.

If everything is too painful, do not make decisions immediately. Give yourself time. Repeat, like Scarlett O'Hara: "I will think about it tomorrow." And for now, just live through the pain. Experience it. And only then decide how to move forward.

Do not let the pain erase everything good that was. Find the strength within yourself to acknowledge that this person did good things, was there for you, supported you. Do not erase this from your memory. We all make mistakes. What matters is what conclusions we draw from them.

Do not destroy children's hearts. Do not transfer your pain to the child. Do not say to them: "Dad left us," "Mom does not love us anymore." The child is not at fault. Do everything to ensure that, in their eyes, both parents remain kind and loving. This is your adult responsibility.

And remember, time heals. It may seem that the pain is unbearable, but it will go away. If you manage to get through this, if your partner helps you through it, your relationship may become even stronger than before. Because you will both understand how costly mistakes can be.

Believe in yourself. In your strength. In the fact that you will manage. And you will manage. Everything will be okay. Just give yourself time.

TEMPTATION, MANIPULATION, PROMISES: HOW MISTRESSES LURE MEN AWAY

In reality, when a man has a mistress, it does not always mean he will leave his family. Men rarely leave their wives for mistresses. However, there are mistresses who skillfully and masterfully manage to lure men away from their families. With patience and cunning, they can destroy a marriage.

We can talk about the strategy that works on a man when he believes he is making the decision himself, when he thinks things with his wife are bad, but everything with his mistress is perfect. Sometimes, he is simply subjected to a well-executed deception, where the woman shows him exactly what he wants to see and behaves exactly how he desires.

Frequent intimate meetings — at least three times a week.

She insists on frequent encounters, making every effort to ensure they happen no less than three times a week. If it is a weekend or a holiday, that is a jackpot for her, because people usually spend these days with their most cherished loved ones. Statistically, having sex three to four times a week is considered normal. In this case, the man gets all the physical intimacy he needs from the mistress. Add to this a romantic setting, and he might even start feeling like he is in love.

Even if a man has a beautiful, fit, and loving wife at home, over time, he starts losing interest. Gradually, sex in the marriage fades. This is how a mistress slowly pulls a man away from his family. She systematically dismantles the foundation of the relationship. It is like pulling the base from a house of cards, making the entire structure collapse. Bit by bit, the man no longer needs his own wife, whom he may have once loved deeply. The mistress can destroy that connection simply by depriving the marriage of its most essential element — intimacy. As the frequency of sex with his wife decreases, emotional tension builds. This creates a vicious cycle: Rising tension in the family leads to fewer intimate moments, and the complete lack of intimacy results in a loss of energetic connection between partners. The tension grows, and feelings seem to fade. The man starts believing that he no longer loves his wife, that he feels more comfortable and happier with the mistress rather than at home.

Then, the family begins to lose weekends and holidays. A smart mistress will do everything she can to pull the man toward her, persuading him to spend weekends together.

Over time, a deep rift forms between the husband and wife. They run out of things to talk about. They no longer share anything in common. Weekends, which are crucial for family bonding, are lost. Why is it so important for families to spend weekends together? Because it recharges them. They talk, hug, kiss — there is an exchange of energy, emotions, thoughts, and shared experiences. Time spent together strengthens the connection and deepens communication.

When a man is with his mistress, they naturally talk about things. There is romance, dates, emotions, new impressions, and passionate sex. He feels alive and happy. Meanwhile, his family gradually fades into the background.

A Shadow Budget Forms

The mistress's goal is to ensure that the man starts financially supporting their relationship—paying for dinners, trips, gifts, and other expenses. He begins investing in her, and naturally, part of his income is hidden from his wife.

The wife senses that something is off. In the past, her husband was more generous—buying gifts, contributing more income, or showing higher business profits. Now, expenses have significantly decreased. She feels tension growing in the family but cannot pinpoint the cause. Meanwhile, with the mistress, things are different—he is willing to invest in that relationship.

The man does not want to give up his secret happiness. He feels comfortable and even starts considering creating a cozy nest. If the mistress has her own place where they meet, he may decide to renovate it or buy things for the home. If she does not have her own space, forcing them to meet in hotels or different locations, the affair is likely doomed. Without a stable love nest, these relationships often fall apart quickly, sometimes without the wife ever discovering the infidelity.

However, if there is a dedicated love nest—a place filled with romance, passion, and emotional connection—the mistress can manipulate the situation further. She sees him off with sorrowful eyes, expressing how much she will miss him, how painful it is to part. Her entire demeanor whispers, "Stay. Stay for good."

Over time, the man finds it harder to leave his "paradise." This is where he feels happy, desired, and free from stress, while at home, tension builds. His wife becomes increasingly frustrated, expressing concerns and making demands. The contrast becomes stark — *paradise here, problems at home.*

The instinct for pleasure often outweighs the instinct for self-preservation. That is why men sometimes leave their families with nothing, running to the mistress, only to realize later that without wealth and status, they are no longer as desirable. Some mistresses strip men of everything, taking advantage of their emotional vulnerability. Blinded by pleasure, they fail to see the financial risks until it is too late.

The mistress is *sickly sweet.* She constantly suffers, hopelessly in love, portraying herself as a woman who never pressures the man and is willing to wait for him *almost a lifetime.* She tells him that she has dreamed of him forever and will wait for him forever, triggering deep emotions in him. She operates on all fronts, sexually and emotionally, creating an environment the man does not want to leave. She builds a cozy *nest* that he perceives as a paradise, a place he no longer wants to walk away from. But this *paradise* can quickly crumble the moment he leaves his family.

Men who establish long-term relationships with mistresses are usually responsible men. An irresponsible man would not tie himself down with a long-term mistress. He would simply move from one woman to another, prioritizing sex without committing to serious side relationships. But a responsible man, often a good family man, does not always seek sex only. Or perhaps it starts that way, but over time, he falls in love and forms an emotional bond with the mistress.

A responsible man does everything *right*. He manages to build and maintain both his first and second families effectively. He invests resources into both, making sure everything is well-structured in each.

A man, through his mistress, begins to realize that he is essentially *stealing time* from her. She loves him, cares for him, and cherishes him. Over time, he may start to feel guilty toward her. She is patient, never rushes him, always welcomes him with a smile and sees him off with warmth. Every meeting with her feels like a celebration, a moment of pure joy. Meanwhile, at home, there are often conflicts and difficulties. At some point, he weighs his options: *his first family or his second family.*

The Mistress's Behavior in a Crisis

Depending on the circumstances and how each participant in the love triangle acts, the situation can develop in different ways. The behavior of the wife, the mistress, and the man himself all play a crucial role.

The Behavior of a Cunning Mistress

Some mistresses, determined to take the man from his family, act discreetly while making sure *not* to portray themselves in a negative light. Their primary goal is to push the wife into ending the marriage *herself*. To achieve this, they may:

- Deliberately create situations that expose the affair (for example, leaving traces such as photos, messages, or subtle hints through third parties).

- Ensure that someone else informs the wife about the mistress's existence.

- Orchestrate "accidental" encounters where the affair becomes undeniable.

The Wife's Reaction and the Development of the Situation

When a wife discovers the betrayal, an emotional explosion is inevitable:

- A heated argument erupts.

- The man is forced to choose: Stay with his family or leave for his mistress.

- Some men, realizing they could lose their wife and children, decide to break things off with the mistress.

- Others, on the contrary, see exposure as a relief and leave for the mistress.

The Mistress's Next Strategy

If the man ultimately chooses to stay with his mistress, she may take different approaches:

- **Playing the victim**, claiming she never wanted to ruin his family, but "things just happened."

- **Displaying "genuine" love and care**, convincing him that life with her will be better.

- **Giving him space to think**, subtly creating an environment where he concludes on his own that she is the best choice.

In such cases, much depends on the man's character, his attachment to his family, and the mistress's ability to manipulate emotions. The outcome varies — some men return to their families, while others leave for good.

The Mistress's Strategy After the Man Leaves His Family

To secure her success and keep the man after he leaves his family, a cunning mistress follows a specific strategy.

1. The Mistress Should Not Become the Wife

The key rule is to maintain the original dynamic of their relationship. If the mistress starts acting like a wife, the man will quickly realize that nothing has changed:

- There was a family before, and now there is another family.

- There were responsibilities before, and now they have appeared again.

- There were problems before, and now they are inevitable again.

At this point, the man starts weighing the pros and cons and may conclude that his wife was actually the better choice.

2. The Phase of Emotional Support

After breaking up with his wife, the man may experience stress and doubts. During this time, the mistress must:

- Provide emotional support.

- Reinforce the idea that he made the right decision.

- Convince him that his wife never appreciated or understood him and failed to create a comfortable environment.

- Emphasize that she, unlike his wife, truly values, loves, and supports him.

3. Creating the Perfect Atmosphere

To contrast herself with the ex-wife, the mistress must present herself in the most appealing way possible:

- Always looking beautiful and well-groomed.

- Cooking delicious meals and creating a cozy environment.

- Avoiding complaints and not demanding anything in return.

- Maintaining an easygoing attitude, free from everyday problems.

At this stage, the man feels happy and reassured that he made the right decision.

4. The Inevitable Crisis

However, over time, the ideal image starts to fall apart:

- It is impossible to pretend forever.

- Household issues and responsibilities eventually arise.

- The man begins to realize that his life has not changed in the way he expected.

This is when many men start to regret their decision and consider returning to their families.

This scheme is a classic strategy used by cunning mistresses to lure men away from their families. They build relationships on contrast—where life with the wife seemed difficult, life with the mistress feels effortless and comfortable. However, this method rarely works in the long run, as reality inevitably takes over.

HOW TO WIN YOUR HUSBAND BACK FROM THE MISTRESS

Let us start with the main question: Why did he leave in the first place?

If you ask the man himself what happened, you will most likely hear:

- "My wife was driving me crazy."

- "There was no sex."

- "She became hard to communicate with."

He found an "escape" in the mistress. But essentially, it is just the novelty effect, like at the beginning of any relationship — everything is bright, fun, romantic. But all of this fades.

It is important to understand: If he left, it does not mean that he is happy there. The novelty will wear off, and she will also have "issues" that he will have to deal with. Over time, all people become themselves.

Now, let us be honest. Do you want him back because:

- You love him?

- You are confident in yourself?

- You want to save the family for the children?

- Or because you are simply feeling bad and lonely right now?

If the reason is just emptiness inside and habit, do not take him back. Instead, focus on yourself. Work on your femininity, self-esteem, and attractiveness. And here is what will happen:

Either your husband will eventually want to come back on his own. Or you will meet a more worthy man, and then, with 80% probability, your ex will want to come back. But you will already say, **"Thank you for leaving. I have someone else now, and I am happy."**

Never try to get someone back if you have not restored your value in their eyes. As long as he sees that you are still willing to forgive him no matter how he behaves, he knows: **"No matter what I do, she will accept me."**

Do you want to change the situation? Stop clinging to him. Think about it: If you had three worthy, reliable, attractive men by your side right now, would you want to go back to the one who betrayed you? Most likely, no.

But as long as you live with the feeling that no one else will love you, you cling to someone who does not deserve to be with you. Do not degrade yourself. Do not beg. Do not lose yourself.

Getting the man back is possible. But only if you first get yourself back — strong, confident, and worthy. Only then will he want to be with you again.

And at that moment, you will already be deciding whether you even need him at all.

How to Win Back a Husband Who Left

If you are asking yourself this question, it is important to admit at this moment, you are the person with whom your man no longer wants to be. He has made his choice. This is painful, but honest. And now you have two paths: Either try to win him back at any cost using tricks and manipulation, or consciously change — for yourself, not for him.

And it is the second path that gives you real chances.

If you really want to win him back, it is important to understand the old scenario no longer works. You cannot stay the same and expect everything to suddenly change. So, the main step is working on yourself.

What does this mean?

- Update your appearance: work on your style, hairstyle, and posture.

- Take care of yourself: go to the gym, visit a salon, attend women's workshops.

- Find a hobby, interest, or creative project.

- Expand your social circle — interact with interesting, new people.

- Develop professionally. Move forward.

The more actively you develop, the more you change, becoming the woman he would want to be with again. It is women like this who men often return to. But it is not a guarantee. However, statistics speak for themselves — in most cases, men do indeed try to return to their ex-wives.

Why? Because:

- With the mistress, the same "domestic routine" starts that was present with you.

- The passion fades, emotions die down, new problems and incompatibility arise.

- The mistress starts to make the same complaints.

- He realizes it is not easy with her either, but you — now you are different.

But there is an important "but." How did you behave when he left? If you:

- Begged, pleaded, humiliated yourself...

- Kept calling, texting, throwing tantrums...

- Insulted him, devalued everything good...

...he will remember you like that. And this will become an obstacle to his return.

Let him go with dignity. Do not scream, do not seek revenge, do not pour out your anger. Let him leave — calmly. Give both yourself and him space.

If he decides to return, it will not happen with a bouquet of roses. He will "test the waters": write, call, ask something. Your reaction is the key.

What to do:

- Do not jump into his arms.

- Do not pour out grievances and accusations.

- Do not make yourself too available.

- Take a pause. Think.

- Let him try to win you back.

Let him feel your value. Let him see that now he must earn your attention. Only then will he be able to truly appreciate you again. There are no guarantees in life. But if you change, you will either win your husband back or meet someone who will truly value you. Work on yourself. Live for yourself. And let him make his own conclusions.

I wish you inner strength, wisdom, and deserving love.

ELIMINATING THE MISTRESS: A STEP-BY-STEP GUIDE

If your husband has been in a long-term relationship with a mistress, what should you do?

Imagine you find out that your husband has a steady mistress, and the relationship has lasted for a year, two, or even longer. This is not a casual fling. It is a relationship that has already taken root, which means there will be no quick solutions.

A man who regularly spends time with the same woman is clearly getting something important out of these relationships. He is already emotionally attached and involved—even if not always consciously. And yes, this will be a struggle that will require patience and endurance on your part.

Step 1. Set Yourself Up for a Long-Term Process

Many women make an emotional leap saying, "I know everything!"—and expect their husband to immediately regret, apologize, end the affair, and everything will go back to the way it was. Unfortunately, that is not how it works. Too much binds him to the other woman. Therefore, it is important to understand from the very beginning: this process will take time. Without understanding this, you will quickly burn out emotionally.

Step 2. Understand Your Husband's Motivation

What led him to this relationship? What was he missing? Often, a man does not fully realize his reasons. But there is always motivation. It could be:

- A lack of a certain type of closeness.

94

- A lack of attention, freedom, or ease.

- A desire for variety, new experiences.

- Dissatisfaction with the emotional background in the family.

Sometimes, this is not about you, but about his internal deficiencies. A conversation on this topic may not be easy, but it is crucial. Without understanding, change is impossible.

Step 3. Begin to Address the Deficit

Once you understand what your husband was lacking, think about how to change that. Not at the expense of yourself, but toward growing the relationship. This may include:

- Shared leisure time, relaxation.

- A new model of family life.

- Changes in the intimate sphere.

- Shared interests, goals, or projects that bring you together.

Perhaps, you need to reconsider the structure of your life, change the usual weekly routine, and include new events and emotional meanings.

Step 4. Stop Constantly Talking About the Mistress

If your husband has ended the affair and is behaving honestly and transparently, it is crucial to stop returning to the topic of the infidelity. Excessive questioning, suspicions, and reproaches only fuel the pain. This prevents you from moving forward. Yes, you are hurt. Yes, you want to know the details. But obsessing over the past kills the possibility of building something new.

Step 5. Set New Common Goals

A family cannot survive just on habit. It requires movement and shared aspirations. You bought an apartment, a car, arranged the household—what is next? When there is no common goal, people get tired of the routine. Especially men, for whom ambitions and achievements are important.

Think of something you can both strive for: travel, hobbies, construction, moving, children's development, or a business. Find a direction that will inspire you both.

These five steps are particularly important if you are dealing not with a fleeting affair, but with a long-term relationship outside of the marriage. It is hard to go through, but it is possible. The key is not to destroy yourself in the process and not to try to solve everything immediately. Patience, clarity, inner support, and readiness for change—these are your foundations.

WHICH INFIDELITIES CAN BE FORGIVEN, AND WHICH CANNOT?

You can forgive infidelity, but you cannot forget it.

Understand this: It will never be the same as before. Even if you forgive, a scar will remain — an emotional wound that can hurt for a long time, and sometimes even forever. The only question is: Can you make the pain fade? Yes, in some cases you can. Let us analyze which situations allow for forgiveness of infidelity and which ones absolutely do not.

1. Cold-Blooded Infidelity ("I Have the Right")

This type is more common among authoritarian men (but it can happen with women too), who are used to putting their interests above everyone else's. These are people who tend to use others as resources. Often, they are diagnosed with antisocial personality disorder.

Sometimes cold-blooded infidelity happens after a life breakthrough such as career growth or becoming rich. The person starts thinking: "I deserve it. Now I have the right to live for myself." They feel they have fulfilled their duties to the family and now they believe they are free. Their actions become rigid and detached, and they accuse you of not providing something.

The prognosis is extremely negative. These people do not change. They will dominate, hide things, and when you try to talk, they will shift the blame to you. This type of infidelity cannot be forgiven. It destroys not only the relationship but also self-esteem.

2. Infidelity Due to Sexual Addiction (Sex Addiction)

This is no longer just an "affair," it is a real addiction, much like drug or gambling addiction. People with this type of infidelity often start with an early interest in pornography and masturbation. They see sex everywhere, sexualize any situation, and cannot regulate their anxiety except through sexual actions.

They may love their partner, understand the value of the relationship, but they cannot stop. They need "release," otherwise, they experience inner tension, breakdowns, and aggression. This is not weakness, it is a psychological illness.

The prognosis is also unfavorable if the person does not realize their problem and does not want to work on it. Only if they acknowledge their addiction, are willing to undergo therapy, and make an effort can they work on themselves.

But if the addiction is not recognized, no matter how good your relationship may be, the likelihood of repeated infidelity will remain. It is like a wormhole—it is inside and can wake up again when stress or pain arises.

3. Burnout or Attempt to "Reach Out"

Unfortunately, sometimes one of the partners tries for a long time to communicate to the other that something is wrong in the relationship: There is a lack of tenderness, attention, respect, and love. He or she feels lonely, devalued. Gradually, resentment or irritation builds up, and internal rejection occurs. A person becomes emotionally "burned out"—inside, there is emptiness. Sometimes, to get some attention, a person may resort to infidelity.

This happens particularly often when the other partner has been ignoring requests for help for years, refuses to discuss problems, does not go to a psychologist or sexologist, claiming: "There is something wrong with you—fix it yourself." Such a position causes accumulated resentment, anger, and ultimately can lead to infidelity as the last straw.

If the infidelity occurred as a reaction to burnout, as a way to end the relationship, and the person subconsciously wants the truth to come out, the prognosis is likely to be negative. In this case, the partner has already emotionally exited the union and is not looking for reconciliation.

But if infidelity is still an attempt to reach out, the last emotional act of desperation, and the partner is ready to meet halfway, work on themselves and the relationship. In this case, there is a chance for recovery. It is important to understand that it all depends on the conditions: Do both partners have the resources, respect, willingness to speak honestly, and listen to each other?

For the most effective way to navigate difficult conversations, read my book *The Simple Formula of Communication.*

4. Romantic Idealism or "Wanting a Fairytale"

This type is often found in people who are generally satisfied with their relationships: "My husband is good, caring, a great father. But in sex, it is boring. Everything is somewhat mundane, not interesting." Or with men: "My wife is a great housewife, a wonderful mother, but there is a lack of emotions, passion, and fire."

Such people begin to search for "magic" elsewhere, often in the form of a passionate, beautiful mistress, in whom they rediscover "that spark," lightness, romance, and the feeling of flying. They chase emotions like a drug addict chasing their first dose, trying to relive the feeling of first love, sometimes not even from these relationships, but from youth or their school love, where everything was "on the rise."

The problem is that this is an infantile strategy. The person does not want to admit that, with age, love becomes different — deeper and more stable, but not as bright and overwhelming. These partners often fantasize or idealize new people, dreaming of "real love," which will always be passionate and unconditional.

If a person does not mature, does not leave this internal childish state, they will change partners, get disappointed, search again, and get disappointed again.

The prognosis can be favorable only in one case: if the person realizes they are chasing a mirage and is ready to work on themselves, grow emotionally, learn to accept reality, and build mature relationships. Only then can closeness be restored, and a truly strong union can be built.

The last two types of infidelity — both from burnout and the desire for a romantic spark — require self-awareness, an honest look inside, and the willingness to change something. If you or your partner are ready for this, then there is a chance not only to save the relationship but to make it deeper and stronger.

5. "Accidentally, the devil made me do it."

Sometimes infidelity happens unconsciously, by accident. For example, at a bachelor party, bachelorette party, company event, wedding, or on a business trip. It all happened, as they say, under the influence, in the moment. Such a person usually deeply regrets it: They are literally ashamed to live, they cannot look you in the eye, and they experience a huge sense of guilt.

No, I am by no means justifying this. If you know that under the influence of alcohol you lose control, be aware of it. Know your weaknesses. And if you are not with your loved one, limit yourself.

But there are cases when a person truly did not plan anything like this. And they come with their head down, in tears, ready to do anything for forgiveness. In such cases, the prognosis can be conditionally positive, with one condition: Both partners must be willing to honestly look at the situation and figure out why it happened.

It is important to understand: Accidental infidelities do not happen out of nowhere. Some trends, tensions, or internal conflicts have already existed. You need to talk about it openly and sincerely. But, of course, this is very painful. Sometimes the person who was cheated on cannot find the resources within themselves to forgive. And this is also normal.

When Infidelity Should Not Be Forgiven

There are clear red flags after which forgiveness can only harm:

Accusations towards you. The cheating partner blames you: "You were not attentive enough," "I warned you," "It is your fault." This shows an unwillingness to take responsibility.

Comparison with the lover. "He kissed me the way you never could," "She is much better than you in bed" — such phrases are unacceptable. This is a low blow, and after such words, it is worth seriously considering: Should you continue?

Complete dishonesty. The cheating partner refuses to be honest: They hide messages, avoid questions, and withhold details. Without openness, trust cannot be restored.

Continued communication with the lover. Even if "we are just colleagues," "there is nothing left," — if the connection is maintained, it is a source of constant stress. Without cutting ties with the old contacts, it is impossible to start something new.

When There is a Chance for Restoration

But there are also positive signals that you should pay attention to:

Deep remorse and empathy. When the partner does not just apologize, but empathizes with your pain, does not brush it off, does not go silent, and does not demand a "quick forgiveness."

Complete transparency. If you ask, they tell the truth. Even if it is bitter. Honesty is the first step to trust.

Willingness to wait and not rush you with forgiveness. The partner does not pressure you, does not ask, "When will you forgive me?" They are there for you but give you space and time.

Infidelity is a powerful trauma. Yes, most couples cannot cope. But there are exceptions. There are couples who became closer after infidelity than they had ever been before. People who had been together for 20 years admitted, "Only now we truly learned to hear each other."

Yes, it is a scar. It remains forever. But if the relationship becomes deeper, more honest, and stronger after it, maybe it was worth it. And if both partners are willing to work on it, there is a chance.

If you are struggling to cope on your own, seek help from psychologists. The most important thing is not to be left alone with your pain.

Whatever your decision may be — to stay, leave, or start over — let it be a conscious, mature decision that leads to your personal happiness.

WHAT SHOULD NOT BE FORGIVEN IN A MAN IN A RELATIONSHIP?

If a woman wants to build a family, if she has small children, if she dreams of motherhood and security, she is likely to forgive a man almost anything. Especially if she has not yet fully realized herself as a mother and strives for stability. This is the reality: For the sake of family, love, and the feeling of having someone by her side, women often endure the unacceptable.

Here are five things that, in my opinion, should never be forgiven in a man:

1. Addictions. Alcoholism, drug addiction, gambling—all of these destroy not only the man but also his partner's life. An addicted person does not live for you or for the family; they live for their addiction. They become dangerous, unpredictable, and incapable of taking responsibility.

2. Chronic irresponsibility. A man who constantly makes promises and does not fulfill them. A man who lets you down in critical moments—when you are sick, when the child is suffering, when support is needed. These are not occasional mistakes; this is systemic behavior. And it is dangerous.

3. Pressure to have an abortion. If a man, without medical indications, insists on terminating the pregnancy, this is a huge red flag. A man should take responsibility for the consequences of intimacy. A child is not just "inconvenient," it is a life. And the man is just as responsible for it as the woman.

4. Violence. Physical, emotional, psychological. Especially towards a woman or children. Even a single act of aggression is a warning signal. With such a person, it is impossible to feel safe. There are no excuses for violence.

5. Passivity and parasitism. When a man strives for nothing, lives off others—most often off the woman or his parents. He shows no initiative and does not take responsibility for his life. This is not a partner; this is a burden.

Of course, everything else depends on the specific situation. Sometimes infidelity can be forgiven, if the man truly realizes his mistake, regrets it, and proves it through his actions.

But the five points above are my personal ranking of things that should never be forgiven under any circumstances. These are not imposed opinions, but conclusions based on my years of practice and observations.

You have the right to have your own criteria. I hope this will help you make a decision that leads to respectful, healthy, and mature relationships.

WHEN TO LEAVE AFTER INFIDELITY

If your partner shows no remorse and seems unconcerned about the pain they have caused you, this is a warning sign. In order for the relationship to survive, your partner must acknowledge how they have hurt you and be willing to take responsibility:

- For their infidelity.
- For your feelings.
- For rebuilding trust.

If they refuse to admit their fault and show no willingness to work on restoring intimacy, these are clear "red flags." A partner who does not regret their actions is, in essence, no longer in a real relationship with you.

Please, read the text above several times.

HOW TO SURVIVE A BREAKUP AND DIVORCE: KEY STEPS TO HEALING

This is truly a difficult and very personal topic. Everyone has their own story and feelings. But one thing is certain — it is important to be able to look at the situation from a slight distance.

Every meeting, every connection with another person is not a coincidence. It is always something meaningful. If we understand why this particular meeting happened or what lesson it brought us, it becomes easier to let go and move forward.

Any relationship is a journey walked together. Even if it was short, it was not in vain. It is important not to devalue this stage, as it holds key meanings and lessons important for both parties.

If you feel a strong emotional attachment, you should ask yourself: Has this connection become an addiction? It is important to understand where it comes from, what lies behind the need to be with someone at any cost. Perhaps it is time to learn inner freedom and rely on yourself.

It is very important to break up consciously — to say everything that has accumulated, not to hold onto resentments, things left unsaid. If you do not share this with your partner, you will have to deal with it with a psychologist years later. Honesty frees and heals.

Do not let others devalue your pain. Statements like "forget it, you will find someone else" only push the feelings inside. This is a dangerous extreme — pretending "it does not hurt." On the surface—strength, inside—unresolved pain that can destroy trust in others over time.

It is important to find a balance. Do not fall into suffering, but also do not pretend everything is fine. Experiencing feelings, seeking support, asking for help is not weakness, it is maturity.

Life does not end with one relationship. Ahead—new meetings, events, emotions. The main thing is to feel, to be alive, and allow yourself to move forward, relying on your experience and strength.

In my book *The Simple Formula for Communication*, I explain how to engage in healthy dialogue, how to identify each partner's needs, and how to express anger constructively. I highly recommend reading it and applying my simple four-step communication formula.

CONCLUSION

Each woman experiences infidelity in her own way. For one, it is the end, for another, it is the beginning of a new version of herself. In this chapter, we discussed which infidelities can be forgiven, when it is time to leave, and when it is time to stand your ground. The decision is always yours, but it is important to remember: Forgiveness is not weakness, but a conscious choice. Leaving is not defeat, but a path to freedom. And eliminating a rival is not revenge, but perhaps a protective reflex, behind which lies a need for love and respect.

The most important thing is not to go against yourself. Do not hold onto a relationship out of fear of being alone. You are not a victim. You are a woman who deserves to be loved, respected, and happy.

CHAPTER 4.

HOW TO LEARN TO TRUST A MAN AGAIN?

Trust is the foundation of any close relationship. But what should you do if it has been broken? How can you trust a man again if, at some point, he let you down or betrayed you? This chapter will help you understand what exactly undermines trust, how to overcome your fears, and how to learn to open up to your partner again. We will talk about practical strategies that strengthen relationships, the possibility of building happiness even after infidelity, and how, step by step, to overcome the crisis and return to inner stability and peace of mind.

STRATEGIES FOR STRENGTHENING TRUST IN RELATIONSHIPS

This section is for those who truly want to save their relationship after infidelity. If you are sure that infidelity cannot be forgiven, my advice may not be relevant for you. And that is fine: Each situation requires an individual approach.

If you have decided to work on restoring the relationship, read this chapter with your partner. The advice here will be for both: for the one who cheated and for the one who was cheated on.

Infidelity is not just a betrayal. For a psychologist, it is primarily a signal of a crisis in the relationship. It is not about bad lovers or the weakness of one of the partners, it is about something gone wrong in your relationship and the system failing.

What does infidelity say about your relationship?

- The relationship in its current form has run its course and requires serious revision.

- One partner was too distant or, on the contrary, too intrusive.

- One partner silenced their needs, the other started seeking their fulfillment elsewhere.

- Sometimes, infidelity is a way (often unconscious) to put an end to something where there is not enough courage for an honest conversation.

Both partners are responsible for the infidelity. Yes, the choice to cheat is the responsibility of the one who cheated. But the other partner often sensed long before the infidelity that something was wrong but turned a blind eye. "I knew that things had become difficult in the relationship. But I did not think it would lead to infidelity."

Path to Recovery. Four Important Steps for the Partner Who Cheated

1.   **Acknowledge the Fact of Infidelity**. Very often, the first thing a person does is deny it. "It is all in your head," they say, even when there is evidence. But without honest acknowledgment, it is impossible to start the recovery. Acknowledgment is the first step, without which trust cannot be restored.

2.   **Transparency and Honesty**. If you want to regain trust, be as transparent as possible. Tell where you go, stay in touch, share passwords, and remove any reasons for doubt. And, of course, any contact with former lovers must be completely cut off. At the same time, it is important not to slip into control, GPS trackers, and ultimatums. This will only push your partner away. Trust is not built on fear, but on openness and voluntary actions.

3.   **Do Not Shut Yourself Off from Questions**. If your partner keeps returning to the topic of infidelity, it is normal. They are in pain, and questions are their way of understanding, living through, and letting go. Do not devalue their feelings: It is better to say, with compassion, that you are sorry for the pain it causes and you want to help.

4.   **An Honest Conversation About the Causes**. It is important to honestly discuss what went wrong in the relationship—without accusations. Not "you gained weight" or "you became cold," but:

- "I felt that we stopped being a couple, and became just parents..."

- "I felt forgotten, unimportant..."

Infidelity is always a personal choice, but the prerequisites may have been on both sides. Understanding them means taking a step towards a new chapter.

Three Tips for the One Who Was Cheated On

1.   **Trust Is Not 0% or 100%**. Think about it: When you first started the relationship, you trusted "in advance." Now,

knowing the person better, trust has fallen to zero. But the truth is, trust can be divided into areas: in one area, it is 90%, in another, 30%. This is normal. And it can be gradually restored.

2.　**Accept That There Is No Absolute Safety**. No one — not the husband, not the wife, not even children — belongs to us completely. And unfortunately, there is no guarantee that infidelity will not happen again. But there is a way out: Clearly state that if infidelity happens again, it will be the end of the relationship. A clear internal boundary gives the brain a sense of control and peace.

3.　**If the Pain Does Not Go Away, It Is Unconscious Protection**. Sometimes we understand everything with our minds, but inside, it feels like a splinter. The pain, anxiety, and fear do not leave. This could be a subconscious way of protecting you, not allowing you to get close again, so you do not experience it all over again.

The most important thing: Have both partners made a conscious decision to stay together? "I want to be with you no matter what. I am ready to work on the relationship."

What potential pitfalls can arise in this process?

Beliefs like "Infidelity is unforgivable" or "We need to stay together no matter what" can hinder you from honestly assessing what you truly want.

The fear of loneliness, shame about a divorce, or the pressure from past experiences (for example, parental stories) can push you towards making the wrong decisions.

A distorted "basic trust in the world" — if you have always felt since childhood that no one is reliable, it will be especially difficult to trust again.

Honest conversations without accusations, about you and your desires, rather than just about daily matters, will help. Discuss what each of you expects from the partner to feel trust again. It should not be vague like "be honest with me," but concrete things: "I want to know where you are when you are late," "It is important for me that we spend the evening together." Find a balance between honesty and a gentle approach. Do not drag out the details of the infidelity, as this will only destroy things. Understand the essence, but do not cause yourself unnecessary pain.

Do not tolerate constant infidelities for the sake of children or public opinion. Relationships based on fear instead of love, rarely bring happiness to anyone.

It is important to understand: Infidelity is not always the end. But it is not always the beginning of a new chapter either. Trust does not return in a week. Usually, it takes six months to a year of honest work and concrete steps. It all depends on both of you. If you want to save the relationship, the path will be long but possible. After infidelity, old relationships "die." You need to build a new form of closeness where both learn to hear each other, communicate their needs and boundaries.

If you cannot manage on your own, consult a family psychologist. A systemic approach helps not only "patch up the hole" but also understand how both of you ended up at this point. Trust can be restored. But it is not about "erasing everything and forgetting." It is about gradually building new, honest, mature relationships — if both truly want this.

HOW TO RESTORE A FAMILY AFTER INFIDELITY: IS HAPPINESS POSSIBLE AFTER BETRAYAL?

Many couples, faced with infidelity, ask the same question: "Can we survive betrayal, save our marriage, and be happy?" As a family psychologist with many years of experience, I can confidently say: Yes, it is possible.

Are there happy families after infidelity? There are hundreds of cases where families not only survived the crisis caused by infidelity but also built new, more mature, and harmonious relationships. Some of these couples, years later, are thankful: "Thank you for everything that happened then. It helped us grow and truly understand each other."

It is important to understand that infidelity is not the end, but rather a symptom that something is wrong in the relationship. The question is whether both partners are ready to work on restoring intimacy.

How does this happen in practice? When a couple comes to see a psychologist, they begin to analyze not just the fact of infidelity, but the entire history of their relationship. And most often, it turns out that there were truly happy periods in the marriage — one, two, three years, during which there was everything: love, sex, trust, common goals, mutual support.

Analyze what exactly the happiness was based on during those times: common leisure, teamwork, a strong circle of friends, emotional intimacy. Then recreate those conditions again but with the current realities and the growth of both partners in mind.

However, if during the work you realize that the marriage was never truly good, the task becomes more complicated: You need to build a family from scratch, but with the same people. This is no longer about "going back to the past," but about forming a new union with new rules, created together.

When is happiness possible after infidelity?

- When both partners acknowledge that something went wrong.

- When both partners are willing to save the family and are ready to act, rather than simply hoping that "everything will somehow get better on its own."

- When the reasons for infidelity are worked through and conflicts are not ignored.

- When new rules for interaction are introduced, taking both partners' interests into account.

- And when both people have the courage to change — for the better.

For couples who seek help, about 80–90% have managed to save their marriages and come out of the crisis stronger. Yes, there are divorces. But they are significantly fewer.

The main rule: Do not return the family to the past — build it anew, but better. Infidelity is not a full stop, but a comma. It is a challenge that can become a new starting point for real closeness. The family should not just "survive" after betrayal. It should change. And if it becomes better, infidelity fades into the past as a painful but passed phase.

ALGORITHM FOR OVERCOMING CRISES IN RELATIONSHIPS: STEPS TO STABILITY AND HAPPINESS

Crises in Relationships: Myth or Reality?

Family life is surrounded by many myths, and one of the most common is that crises in marriage are inevitable. It is often said that if conflicts arise and intimacy fades, you should look at the calendar: "Oh, it is our five-year anniversary! Crisis, it is just the right time!" And then all that is left to do is wait for it to "pass."

But is it really like that? Let us take a closer look.

Where did the theory of "crisis years" come from?

In the past, the concept of crises had real significance. People married between the ages of 18–20, often moved in with their parents, and quickly had children. In the conditions of close living quarters and limited resources, this created tension and arguments.

- 3-year crisis—the birth of the first child, fatigue, lack of sleep and money, absence of sex.

- 7-year crisis—the second (or lack of the second) child, changing roles, accumulation of dissatisfaction.

- 10-year crisis—as people approach 30, they begin to think, "Am I missing something?" and may start seeking new sensations.

But times have changed. People now marry later, often live separately from their parents, and approach having children more consciously. Everything has become more individualized.

New Realities — New Crises

Today, crises in a couple are more related to age stages and changes in life priorities, rather than the length of the marriage.

- At 30: both men and women experience an increased sexual drive, but this is often ignored in the relationship.

- Around 40: a feeling that "life is passing by," a desire to "try something else."

- At 50: men experience decreased activity, women undergo physiological changes (menopause), which affect sexual life and psychological well-being.

Can You Prepare for a Crisis? Yes. Here are 5 key tips

1. Maintain Sexual Intimacy

Do not let intimacy fade. Sex is not just about physiology, but also about emotional connection. If there is no sex, there is a high risk of growing apart. Both men and women need regular intimacy. Yes, both should want it. But sexuality does not disappear on its own — it fades in places where it is not nurtured.

2. Create Family Leisure

Without pleasures and outings, life turns into routine. It is important to go to cafes, movies, travel, even if it is just to nature. Find time for each other, especially on weekends. Plan your leisure in advance — do not leave it for "later."

3. Take Care of Your Appearance

Appearance matters. Not for the gloss, but for the feeling of your own attractiveness. Get a check-up every five years: skin, hair, teeth, body. Take care of yourself not out of obligation, but for your own comfort and pleasure. By the way, regular sex is the best motivation to take care of yourself!

4.   Have Common Goals

Family is not just about "living together," it is about going towards something together. Bought an apartment, paid off the mortgage, then what? Have the goals ended? Find new ones: Build a summer house, move, start a joint project, have another child, or take a dream trip. The key is to pursue goals together.

5.   Share Interests

If one partner develops a new hobby and the other ignores it, the couple starts drifting apart. If your husband gets into fishing, running, or cycling, join him, at least sometimes. Shared hobbies bring you closer than any "heart-to-heart talks."

Women's circles, esoterics, astrology — these can be interesting, but they should not replace communication with your husband.

Crises exist, but they can be prevented. Crises are not a sentence. They are transitional phases that can be prepared for. If in your relationship there is intimacy, leisure, self-care, common goals, and shared hobbies — no crisis will scare you. A family is like a garden: If you water it, feed it, and take care of it, it will bloom.

HOW TO KEEP LOVE: 8 KEY RULES FOR HEALTHY RELATIONSHIPS

In this chapter, we will discuss 8 basic rules for healthy relationships — those that not only help create closeness but also maintain it in the long term. Even if your relationship seems perfect right now, these principles can serve as excellent prevention for future difficulties.

1. Realistic, not ideal, expectations

Each of us has an image of the "ideal partner." But in real life, we meet a living person with their complexities and contradictions. Healthy relationships are when you accept your partner as they are, without trying to reshape them into your own template.

2. The ability to argue is a plus

Conflicts are normal. Everyone has them. It is important not to avoid them, not to suppress discontent, but to learn how to discuss, reconcile, and move forward. It is like a skill — the more you practice, the easier it becomes.

3. Trust and clarity

When there is trust in a relationship, there is no need to guess, check, or feel tense. It saves a lot of energy. If trust is shaken, do not let it slide, work on it. Without trust, there is no healthy relationship.

4. Be honest with yourself first

Do not pretend everything is fine if you feel anxious inside. Do not ignore the "warning signs." True sincerity starts with honesty with yourself—only then will real openness with your partner develop.

5. Do not suppress resentments

If something bothers you, talk about it sincerely, calmly and directly. Do not keep it inside. Accumulated resentment can lead to serious breakdowns. Communication is the key to emotional comfort in a couple.

6. Personal space

Everyone should have their own space. Their own friends, interests, hobbies, time alone. If you can enjoy life separately and together become even happier—this is a mature relationship.

7. Joy from time together

When you enjoy just being together, even in silence, it is one of the signs of harmony. Comfort, trust, the feeling that you are "on the same wavelength"—these are important components of emotional intimacy.

8. Be friends with each other

A friend is a person with whom it is safe to be yourself. With whom you can talk about anything without fear of being judged. If you feel like your partner is your best friend, this is not only a healthy relationship, but it is happiness.

Trust is not an instant feeling but the result of a conscious choice, consistent steps, and mutual readiness to work on the relationship. Even after betrayal, it is possible to restore closeness if both partners are willing to meet each other halfway. Learn to talk about your feelings, set clear boundaries, and give yourself time. Remember: Restored trust can be even stronger than before if it is built on maturity, honesty, and love.

WHERE IS YOUR DESIRE? TEN HIDDEN CAUSES OF LOW LIBIDO IN WOMEN

There are two main issues that people most often bring to a sexologist: the first is the absence of orgasm, and the second is the lack of desire for sex.

Cause number zero. Yes, we start with this one — your unrealistic expectations about your own capabilities. This often happens when a person does not understand what sexual constitution is. Simply put, it is your sexual temperament. It is individual and varies from person to person. It is completely normal to either want sex frequently or not want it at all.

Some people genuinely have little to no desire for sex, and that does not mean they have a problem. At the same time, there are those who want sex four or more times a day, and that is also normal. Unrealistic expectations arise from a lack of information — you simply do not know what amount of sex is normal for you. Should you be feeling desire every day, or is once a week more natural? You may not be aware of your own sexual temperament.

Perhaps, in the past, you wanted sex more often — maybe in your younger years, when sexual desire naturally peaks, or at the beginning of a new relationship, when sexual attraction is heightened. But those periods are not indicative of your baseline libido. The initial hormonal surge typically fades after a year or a year and a half, and after that, people settle into a pattern that aligns with their true sexual temperament.

That is why, in long-term relationships, people often say, "I used to want sex more often; I think back then, the amount was normal, but now something must be wrong with me." When you start digging into the reasons, you may realize that nothing is actually wrong, that your libido has not decreased. So, unrealistic expectations are cause number zero.

What is the most important starting point when we are not talking about decreased libido?

Determine your sexual constitution. Find out what stage of a relationship you are in. Has the honeymoon phase passed, or is it still ongoing? Take a look at your lifestyle. If there have not been any sudden health issues, no major life changes, and no serious stress, and you have simply settled into a sexual rhythm that feels natural for you, then everything is fine.

It is important to understand that sexual desire is not the same as thirst or hunger. Many people assume that because sex is an instinct, it should work similarly, meaning that at some random moment, you should suddenly be struck by the urge to have sex. When we think about instincts, we imagine that they should naturally make themselves known.

Yes, people with a strong sexual constitution do experience spontaneous desire. They may indeed be walking somewhere and suddenly realize they want sex. But not everyone is wired this way. Expecting desire to suddenly hit you out of nowhere and compel you to masturbate or have sex is completely unrealistic. The idea that sexual desire should function like thirst is simply inaccurate.

If you expect to feel the urge for sex the same way you feel hunger or thirst, you might find yourself just waiting and waiting. Perhaps, during ovulation, women may experience temporary spikes in desire and turn to their partner, but in the end, you might end up at a sexologist's office saying, "I only want sex once a month."

In reality, you likely want it more often; you just do not recognize the signs of your own desire. Your expectations may be too high. Unrealistic expectations often stem from a lack of accurate information about what libido is, how it works, and from being overly demanding of yourself.

Comparing sexual desire to hunger or thirst, expecting that you should suddenly feel an overwhelming urge to relieve sexual tension right now, is misleading. Yes, this happens in people with a strong sexual constitution, but for most people, it does not work that way.

Now, let us determine what low libido is.

We know the following about decreased libido: A person experiences distress due to a lack of sexual desire, and this distress persists for more than two months. That is the key factor.

So, if someone used to want and enjoy sex but then lost interest, yet does not feel distressed about it, we cannot say they have a problem. It is not up to a non-specialist to decide what constitutes a problem. It is not for someone else to tell you that you *should* be having sex two or three times a week or that you *must* feel sexual desire at a certain frequency. That logic simply does not work.

We always start with what a person really wants. As I mentioned earlier, wanting sex is normal, and not wanting sex is also normal.

So, if you feel like you might have an issue, first check your expectations. Are they realistic? Are you holding yourself to some external standard? Get the right information first. Then, if you discover actual reasons that might be lowering your libido, you can start addressing them.

Ask yourself right now: Are you satisfied with how often you want sex? Not your friends, not people online — you. If the answer is *yes*, then let it go. You are perfectly fine.

Now we can talk about the real reasons behind decreased libido.

1. Sex Is Simply Unpleasant for You

Ask yourself:

"What does sex mean to me? Is it pleasure? Enjoyment? Orgasms? Intense emotions? Or is it just routine? Discomfort? Pain? Irritation?"

It might seem like sex is pleasurable for everyone, but that is not the case. Some people associate sex with pain and discomfort. This often happens when a person has forced themselves to engage in sex when they did not want to, whether to avoid conflict, please a partner, or because they felt obligated.

- A woman might have experienced pain during sex but stayed silent, fearing it would ruin the moment.

- She might have had sex while not aroused, leading to discomfort.

- After childbirth, many women experience physical changes that make sex painful.

- During menopause, hormonal shifts can make sex uncomfortable, turning it into something dreadful rather than pleasurable.

- Some people engage in sexual practices they do not actually enjoy, like agreeing to anal sex when they do not truly want it.

When these experiences accumulate, a person may start associating sex with something unpleasant, leading to avoidance and a natural suppression of desire. It is completely logical that if your experience with sex has been painful or uncomfortable, your libido will decrease.

I want to emphasize that this is the first reason to consider. It might seem logical to start by looking into physical health — getting hormone tests, seeing a gynecologist, etc. However, before that, we need to examine a person's attitude toward sex.

For example, if someone previously enjoyed sex, found it pleasurable, and then suddenly stopped wanting it, the next step would be to ask: "How do you feel about sex now?"

- If they respond, "Great, positive, I love sex", then yes, it makes sense to check with an endocrinologist or gynecologist to rule out any medical conditions affecting libido.

- But if they say, "To be honest, I never really liked sex. I do it just for my partner. He likes anal sex, but it is painful and uncomfortable for me, yet I never say anything."

- Or "I have had a negative experience in the past, and whenever I think about sex, I just do not want it at all."

- Or "I am afraid of sex because I had a bad experience that led to an infection or other consequences."

These responses indicate a deep association between sex and discomfort or negativity.

People in this situation often feel isolated because they are surrounded by those who genuinely enjoy sex. When they express their lack of interest, they often face pressure and judgment: *"What do you mean you do not like sex? That is not normal! Sex is amazing! How can you not enjoy it?"*

Hearing this, they tend to shut down further and avoid intimacy even more.

What can you do in this situation?

- Identify the root cause of why you feel this way about sex and work on addressing it.

- Consider the impact of psychosexual development and ingrained beliefs about sex.

- Maybe you grew up in an environment where sex was shamed — your parents told you it was dirty, sinful, or wrong.

- If so, you might have internalized these beliefs, forming a deep-seated idea that sex equals something bad.

- In this case, the key is to work through and reframe these learned perceptions.

2. No Time for Sex – No Sex

Going back to where we started: expecting desire to arise on its own.

Anyone in a long-term relationship will understand this well. When you have been with your partner for a long time, living side by side, you always have the opportunity to have sex. You know you can do it tomorrow, the day after, or next week. And at some point, you realize that sex has become rare — maybe just once a month.

Why? Because you do not make time for it.

This is a false reason for low libido — you are simply not paying attention to the fact that there is no dedicated space for intimacy in your schedule. You have a million things to do, and by the end of the day, there is just no time left.

If you expect that you should suddenly feel a strong desire, stop everything, and go have sex, you are likely to struggle. You might even think, *"My libido is low,"* when in reality, it is not.

There is a practice called **"libido tracking."** More details on how to do this are in the next chapter. This exercise helps you notice when your desire actually arises.

After two weeks of tracking, people often realize:

- Desire does come up.
- It comes in the morning, at work, in the evening.
- It is not just *once a month!*

So look at your schedule. Look at your lifestyle.

Ask yourself: *"Is there even room for sex in my daily routine?"*

Some may react: "*Oh no, scheduling sex? That is ridiculous! Sex should be spontaneous!*"

Sure. For some, sex must be spontaneous. But then accept that it will only happen once a month. You have to choose. On the other hand, nothing stops you from having spontaneous sex even when you have a schedule! You can **break the plan!** If you do not like the word "schedule," call it a date. Think about it — when you were building your relationship, you went on dates and prepared for them, including mentally preparing for sex. It felt natural. But once we live together, somehow this stops being normal. Setting up date nights and mentally tuning in for sex works great. It helps awaken your libido and bring attention back to it. Because we simply forget about it.

3. You Simply Have No Energy for Sex

You know that feeling when you kind of want it, you even planned for it, but you are just too exhausted?

You lie down and think, *"Maybe not today."*

It is important to find a time when you still have enough energy for sex. This also affects your sexual responses — arousal and orgasm. It is harder to get turned on or reach orgasm when you are physically drained.

Some might mistake this for low libido, but that is not the case. The issue is not a lack of desire; it is just that you do not have the energy for it at that moment.

Try tracking when your natural desire tends to be strongest. Pay attention:

- Are you more in the mood in the morning?

- Does your desire peak in the afternoon?

- Or do you feel it more in the evening?

Use this self-awareness to your advantage.

4. Pregnancy and Postpartum Period

During pregnancy, desire can fluctuate dramatically from *"I want you more than ever"* to *"Do not come near me."* These waves are completely normal, and there is no need to worry about them.

After childbirth, low libido is more common. There are two main reasons for this:

1. **Physical exhaustion.** A new mother is busy with the baby and simply does not have the energy for sex.

2. **Hormonal changes.** Prolactin, the hormone responsible for lactation, naturally suppresses libido.

The most challenging time is usually the first six months postpartum. After that, a woman gradually starts feeling like herself again, and her desire returns.

However, it should not take years. As you reduce breastfeeding, your libido should gradually come back. If you notice that you are breastfeeding less and less, but your desire is not returning, then the issue likely lies elsewhere, and you may need to consult a sexologist. Do not delay it. Do not wait two or three years for your libido to magically "wake up." Find the cause and actively work on reviving your sexual desire.

This brings us back to reason one — if, during this period, you force yourself to have sex despite feeling uncomfortable or repulsed by it, you complicate the situation even more. You start associating sex with:

- Pain.

- Discomfort.

- Irritation.

- A sense of duty rather than pleasure.

This is how a negative association with sex forms. And once it becomes deeply ingrained, it is much harder to reverse. Do not let it get to that point.

5. Relationship Issues

Some people look for answers in their health, getting hormone tests, checking for imbalances, but if you and your partner fight like cats and dogs, if you are hurt, unhappy, or experiencing any form of abuse (emotional, physical, financial), then the problem is most likely not hormonal. The issue is that you do not want this specific partner right now.

That does not mean you will never want them again. Periods of conflict can pass, and your desire may return. But in the present moment, when the relationship is strained, a decrease in attraction is completely normal.

Instead of blaming your libido, address the actual problem:

- Seek couples therapy.

- Have honest conversations.

- Find ways to resolve your conflicts.

Men too, often expect that their arousal should happen instantly. They assume that the moment a woman undresses, they should immediately want her. But what if, just moments before, she said something deeply hurtful? That emotional impact matters. Men are not machines with a switch that automatically triggers an erection. Emotional states affect desire and ignoring that is a mistake.

6. Sex Is Boring

Sometimes, everything in your relationship is great. You love each other, live a healthy lifestyle, feel desire, and even masturbate. But when you think about having sex, you feel uninterested — it is always the same routine. It is boring.

This leads to avoiding sex, not because your libido is low, but because the sex itself is uninspiring. It is repetitive, predictable, and does not excite you anymore. You already know exactly what will happen, and that kills the thrill.

Sometimes, you may even notice that orgasms feel dull. They happen, but they are not as intense or satisfying as they used to be. Arousal becomes harder, and you start subconsciously avoiding sex while looking for reasons elsewhere.

Ask yourself:

- Does your sex life excite you?
- Is it still interesting?
- Has it become routine and uninspiring?

If the answer is yes, it is time for change. Life is full of other exciting, pleasurable activities, and if sex is not enjoyable, you will naturally prioritize something else.

7. Chronic Illness and Medications

Certain health conditions and medications can affect libido. If you noticed a drop in sexual desire after starting a new medication, it is worth discussing with your doctor.

Many people feel embarrassed to bring this up, but it is a valid concern. In some cases, your doctor may be able to adjust the dosage or switch the medication to help restore your libido.

However, in some situations, there is no alternative, and you may just need to wait it out. If that is the case, be patient and remind yourself that this is temporary.

8. Stress

If you recognize the factors that increase stress, try to minimize their impact on you. When you are already experiencing stress, focus on actions that help you manage and reduce it. Find methods that effectively lower your stress levels. It is very useful to identify what specifically triggers stress in you. Stress can affect your desire, and typically, this influence lasts for about six months, especially after a significant stressful event. Support yourself with knowledge, a healthy lifestyle, and over time, your desire will gradually return. Try to avoid returning to the same lifestyle that contributed to a decrease in libido in the first place.

9. Intense Exercise

If your workouts are so intense that you have no energy left for sex, this could be the issue. The solution is straightforward — reduce the intensity or frequency of exercise, and you will regain the energy for intimacy.

10. Insomnia and Poor Sleep

I highly recommend learning about sleep hygiene and understanding how it works. When you sleep well and get high-quality rest, and when you eliminate sleep-related myths, your overall life quality improves. You will have more strength and energy. If you also improve your diet and incorporate regular physical activity, you will notice your desire awakening and becoming stronger. Sleep and sex are deeply interconnected.

In summary, pay attention to your expectations and self-imposed demands. Try the "My Libido" exercise to develop awareness of your sexual desire. Evaluate whether there is room for sex in your daily routine and adjust your sleep schedule and diet if you recognize that they are affecting your libido.

EXPLORE YOUR PASSION: A PRACTICE FOR AWARENESS AND IDENTIFYING LIBIDO-BOOSTING FACTORS

The "Libido Tracking" exercise: a practice for awareness and identifying libido-influencing factors. The **"Libido Tracking"** exercise is a sexology-based technique aimed at developing awareness of sexual desire. It helps to better understand libido dynamics, recognize its natural fluctuations, and identify factors that influence it.

How to Perform the Exercise

Keeping a Journal. For **2–4 weeks**, record daily:

1.   Your libido level on a scale from **1 to 10**.

2.   Time of day when desire arises (morning, afternoon, evening, night).

3.   Thoughts, emotions, or circumstances that preceded changes in libido.

4.   Physical sensations related to sexual attraction.

5.   Factors that increased or decreased libido (stress, fatigue, exercise, nutrition, social interactions, etc.).

Analyzing the Collected Data

- Are there patterns? For example, does libido increase at a specific time of day or in particular situations?

- Is there a correlation between libido levels and factors like stress, physical activity, or diet?

- How do emotional states (joy, anxiety, fatigue) affect sexual desire?

Conclusions and Self-Regulation

After analyzing your data, you can:

- Adjust your lifestyle to enhance the quality of your sex life.

- Develop greater awareness and accept natural libido fluctuations without guilt or anxiety.

- Identify psychological or physiological barriers if libido is unstable or decreasing.

Who Can Benefit?

- Individuals experiencing libido fluctuations (increased/decreased desire).

- Those who want to better understand their body and sexuality.

- Couples looking to synchronize their desires.

- People going through stress or hormonal changes.

This is a simple yet effective practice that helps improve understanding and regulation of sexual desire.

CHAPTER 5.

PRACTICAL STEPS FOR ENDING A RELATIONSHIP

Ending a relationship is not just parting ways with a person, but a deep internal process that requires honesty, strength, and awareness. This chapter will help you understand whether to fight for love or let it go. You will learn how to determine when a relationship has run its course, how to break up with respect for yourself and others, and how to let go of the past without destroying yourself. Here, you will find strategies to help you endure the pain, maintain your dignity, and prepare your heart for new feelings.

2 METHODS TO MAKE THE RIGHT DECISION: STAY OR LEAVE?

The pandemic became a trigger for many divorces. Why did this happen? It's simple: People found themselves trapped together 24 hours a day for an extended period. In isolation, old resentments, unspoken conflicts, and accumulated grievances surfaced. For the first time in a long while, couples were confronted with them face-to-face. And what to do with it—no one knew. Leave? Stay? Without therapy or attempts at reconciliation, the only solution many people saw was to separate.

Many couples have lived for decades in a familiar but unconscious pattern: once emotions flared, they got married and had children. Then came the daily routine, work, responsibilities. He is at work, she is with the kids or vice versa. Sometimes they argue, sometimes they make up, but real contact is no longer there. There is no intimacy. There is no trust. Everything seems to run on autopilot. They live like neighbors.

The pandemic merely uncovered a reality that people had previously preferred to ignore. It opened their eyes to the fact that relationships lacked what makes them alive. Someone got tired of being silent and began to speak out. Someone realized they had not felt happiness with their partner in a long time. For the first time in a long while, the truth came out.

And now you stand at a crossroads: Stay or leave?

It is important to understand that what you are facing now is not new. You have been living with this all along. It is just that before, there was no opportunity or courage to acknowledge it. But now it is impossible to ignore. Yet, it is from this point that growth begins.

You can choose two paths:

- Stay and learn to live in a new way, honestly, with respect for your own and others' feelings.

- Leave, if you understand that continuing is no longer possible.

But before making a sudden decision, give yourself time. Do not rush. Live through your feelings. Understand what you really want. It often seems like leaving is easier. But staying, experiencing, and overcoming — this is what creates true closeness and unity.

If you choose to stay, start with the most important thing, an open conversation. Confess to yourself and your partner what you are missing, what causes you pain. Not in the form of accusations, but from the first person: "I miss...", "It hurts when...". It may be uncomfortable, but this is the way to true closeness. For more on how to conduct difficult conversations, read my book *The Simple Formula of Communication.*

A good practice is to write down your needs and read them to each other. If possible, do this with a therapist. If not, do it on your own. You can even play a game: switch roles. Imagine that you are your partner. What is it like for him to be with you? What emotions is he experiencing? This simple exercise can give many insights.

After this, it is important to acknowledge: "Yes, I can be difficult," "I understand that it is hard for you too." This gives the other person a sense of support and understanding. Trust emerges.

And then, agreements. What can we do to make things easier? What am I willing to change? And what am I not?

If you have decided to break up, observe yourself in new relationships. Because everything that was not dealt with in the past will inevitably show up again. And to avoid repeating the same scenario, it is important to notice in time: "I am silent again," "I am tolerating again." Only awareness will help build new, healthy relationships. Do not blame others. Look at yourself. This is an invitation to personal growth. The question is not what happened, but what you will do with it now.

To Break Up or Not? The Scenario Method

The question "to break up or not" is one of the most pressing and relevant for many. Every person has moments of doubt: Is it worth continuing this relationship, or is it time to let go? How can you understand what is true? How can you resolve the internal conflict?

The difficulty of this question is that there is simply no universal answer. In every couple, there is their own history, their own nuances, their own pains. Therefore, it is important not to look for templates but to work through your specific situation.

Why is it so difficult?

When a person cannot make a decision, it is almost always a battle between two motivations. Doubts torment: Stay or leave? The internal swings are exhausting. Half the day, you live with the thought "we will be together," and then something happens, and you already imagine the breakup. As a result, stagnation occurs. There is a feeling inside that you are treading water, while life is passing you by. This is especially painful if you are young, full of energy and feelings, then suddenly stuck in limbo.

Often behind this is fear, people are not so much holding on to the relationship, as they are afraid of breaking up. They do not even allow themselves to think about it. But in essence, the choice is not between "breaking up or staying," but between "staying in a relationship with unresolved conflicts" and "facing the unknown after a breakup."

Conflicts are normal

It is important to understand that conflicts exist in any relationship. This is natural. People are different, interests, needs, and even habits too. Some disagreements are easily resolved, others take time. But some drag on for years and still find no resolution.

This is normal, but here is what is important: Any conflict is a potential point of growth or destruction. Relationships in which the possibility of breaking up is ignored become unwholesome. To truly understand what you want, it is important to imagine both scenarios: not just to save the relationship but also to break up.

How can you understand what to do?

Do an experiment — mentally "plan" your breakup. Yes, exactly like that. Write down how it might happen. What will happen next? Where will you live? How will your daily life, emotions, and rhythm of life change?

This does not mean that you are necessarily going to leave. This "rehearsal" helps to see the reality. Right now, you are comparing a familiar, albeit painful, situation with the frightening unknown. But if the breakup scenario becomes clearer, it will be easier and more honest to decide.

It is also important to think through the scenario in which you stay together. What could the way out of the crisis look like? What are you willing to change? What compromises are you willing to make? What do you want to achieve together?

It is this comparison of two specific scenarios that helps you understand which path is more honest and healthier for you.

To Stay or Leave the Relationship: the Method of Small Steps

When such a question arises, it is always a sign of a crisis. Because if everything were simple, decisions would come quickly. For example, there are easy everyday arguments that do not cause any doubts: "Well, everyone argues." Or, on the contrary, something shocking happens, and it becomes obvious you need to leave. In that case, everything is clear, and the decision is made instantly.

But most often, people live in doubt for a long time. And then the most difficult thing arises — the internal struggle of motivations. When the pros and cons of the relationship are roughly balanced. When what you are getting is almost equal to what you are not getting.

Why is it so difficult to make a decision?

Let us imagine a woman who is in a relationship with a man but does not feel happy. She talks to him about her feelings, but either he does not understand, does not want to listen, or is unable to. Perhaps he shows narcissistic traits, manipulates emotions, ignores, cheats, or has addictions.

The woman is tired and can no longer live like this. But at the same time, she does not know how to change the situation. She understands clearly that she does not want it this way. But how she wants it, she does not know.

This is the crisis point.

What can she do in such a situation?

The first and most important thing is to acknowledge that you cannot decide right now. This is not your weakness but simply a fact. Perhaps you are being held back by finances, children, pressure from relatives, or internal beliefs like "you cannot destroy the family."

You feel like you are stuck: You cannot leave, but staying like this is unbearable.

Here is what you need to do:

1. Make two lists:

The first list is what important things you are getting in this relationship (for example: financial or physical security, emotional closeness, feeling of family, status, care, father figure, etc.).

The second list is what you would do immediately after a breakup, things you currently cannot allow yourself to do. For example: join a gym, meet friends more often, start a new career.

It is important not to rush the decision. Just notice: right now, you cannot make it. And that is okay. Set a "review date" for yourself — in a month, three months, or six months.

2. Keep living — but differently

While you are still in the relationship, start slowly moving toward the life you want. You do not need to wait for a final decision to begin taking care of yourself now.

Develop, learn, meet people, fulfill your desires. Do not spend any more energy trying to change your partner if they are not listening. Instead, make agreements with yourself.

There is no right answer to the question "Should I stay or leave?" There is only your path. The most important thing is not to be afraid to face the truth and make decisions from an adult position, not from fear or guilt.

Take care of yourself and your loved ones. And be happy — no matter how your relationship turns out.

You can find more decision-making techniques in the book *How to Deal With a Love Triangle: The Simple Guide to Overcoming Betrayal, Getting Out of Toxic Cycles and Taking Control of Your Relationship Choices.*

HOW TO UNDERSTAND THAT YOUR RELATIONSHIP HAS NO FUTURE, AND IT IS TIME TO BREAK UP

This question concerns many people, especially women, because they are more likely to think, doubt, and experience inner turmoil. Sometimes, the mere fact that you cannot find a clear answer starts to poison life and destroy the relationship from within.

Doubts are normal. The future is not pre-programmed. If you feel completely confident that you know how your relationship will turn out, it is likely an illusion. We cannot predict everything because there are too many variables.

But if you and your partner are trying to see a shared future, discussing it, sharing thoughts, and still cannot find common ground, then perhaps, at this moment, that future really does not exist for you. And it is important to acknowledge that.

Sometimes the question of the future is an attempt to avoid answering about the present. If the relationship exists only in messages or is based on "someday" statements: "He will get a divorce," "He will get a job," "The children will grow up" — this is not real. This is waiting. And the question "what will happen next" becomes a way not to see that right now, there is nothing.

There is also the situation where you have already decided to break up, but cannot bring yourself to do it. Rational reasons "for" breaking up sound convincing, but the reasons "against" are vague: "What if," "What will people say," "We promised."

This is a typical internal conflict: Living like this is no longer possible, but the alternative is scary or unclear.

An important marker is how you feel in the relationship. If during this relationship you have become more anxious, unhappier, more depressed, or feel that you have lost yourself – this is a warning sign. Happiness is not just "everything is formally fine." It is an inner feeling.

If you are constantly waiting for changes from your partner, but they do not happen… He says, "everything will get better when…" but does not act. This is avoidance of responsibility. A relationship is built by two adults, each of whom can and wants to invest. If only one promises, it is a dead-end.

If you cannot honestly say that you love this person… If your feelings are undefined, if you are together more out of "habit," fear of being alone, or because "it is more convenient" – this is not the foundation for a happy future. It is a path to dependence and disappointment.

If you take everything upon yourself and drag the relationship for both of you… When you are the "engine" of the relationship, and your partner is passive or completely ignores what is happening, this is also a warning sign. A relationship should be a partnership, not the management of one adult for two.

If you are together only for sex… There is no magic in "it will get better with time." Sex without emotional connection and mutual effort does not turn into a serious relationship on its own.

Love is not control or saving someone. Do not build a relationship with the expectation that "he will change." People change rarely, and if they do, it is by their own will, not from the fear of losing you, not because you insist.

Be honest with yourself.

HOW TO BEHAVE WITH AN EX: 4 STRATEGIES FOR MAINTAINING INNER PEACE

Breakups are an important topic. In our culture, unfortunately, there is no clear scenario for how to behave after a relationship ends. We are used to the fairy tale ending: "...and they lived happily ever after." But life is more complicated, and it continues after the "end."

How can a woman behave after a breakup? There are four common scenarios. Let us talk about each one, and the typical mistakes to avoid.

Scenario 1: "Let us stay friends" This sounds harmless, but in reality, it is a trap. When you break up, you experience a loss. And continuing communication while you are in the process of "letting go" means not fully going through the breakup. A conflict arises in your mind: "We broke up, but we are still talking." This prevents you from moving on.

Maintaining neutral, polite relationships is possible, especially if you share children, work, or mutual friends. But true friendship immediately after a breakup is practically impossible for a healthy person. The exception is psychopaths, who are generally incapable of attachment.

Scenario 2: "We are not together, but from time to time..." Sex with an ex is another trap. Often, this is explained as: "It is convenient," "It is safe," "We know each other." But in reality, every act of intimacy reignites an emotional connection. This means you are not free. These "no-strings-attached" relationships are a myth, especially if deep down you still think about him, still feel for him. If you have decided to stay in such a relationship, it is important to honestly admit: You are still connected. And do not deceive yourself into thinking it is "just sex."

Scenario 3: "I do not need a relationship anymore" Sometimes after a painful experience, a woman decides: "That is it. Relationships are not for me. I am alone." And this can be the right path. But only if it is a mature, conscious decision made after experiencing the pain, not running away from it. If it is just fear of feeling pain again, it is not freedom, but a block. Sooner or later, a breakdown will happen: a call to the ex, a casual affair, and everything will repeat.

Scenario 4: "He is dead to me" A woman completely blocks the ex: on social media, the phone, everywhere. It seems like the end. But in reality, she continues to watch him, seeking confirmation that he is suffering without her. This is not a finished relationship, it is "living with the ex in your mind." This approach drains energy and time, prevents you from building something new, and makes it difficult to be happy. He is still inside, even if masked as "I do not think about him."

The only way out is one: to truly end it. To truly finish a relationship, you need to:

- Make a final decision.
- Say everything you wanted to — both the good and the bad.

- Forgive each other, if possible. And ask for forgiveness for your part.

- Say goodbye. Not "see you later," but "goodbye forever."

Then the ex becomes just a person from the past. The same as thousands of other passersby. And only then can you truly free yourself and move on.

HOW TO LET GO OF THE PAST AND OPEN YOUR HEART FOR NEW RELATIONSHIPS

Why is it so hard to let go of the past? Why, even after ending a relationship, do we continue to mentally return to it, suffering and losing the chance for present happiness?

A woman may live for a long time in memories. And even if the mind says, "It is over," the heart continues to cling to the image, hope, and dream. Often, this happens not because love is still alive, but because something was left unfinished. Or because it is scary to look into the future, where there is no clear scenario yet.

Past relationships leave a mark on us. Sometimes it is a warm memory, sometimes it is a wound that does not heal for a long time. Even after breaking up, we often mentally return to the past, reconsidering events, fantasizing about "what would have happened if…". This is natural. But when the past becomes an anchor that prevents us from building the present, it is time to say goodbye.

Why do we get stuck in the past? There are two main reasons:

1. The emotional aftermath of the breakup. After a breakup, we miss the routine, the habits, even the arguments. We long not so much for the person, but for the feeling of closeness, even if it was painful. Sometimes this is accompanied by feelings of guilt if we were the ones who initiated the breakup or resentment if we were betrayed. But in any case, the longing is always there.

2. Fear of the future. The past, however it was, is familiar. The future is not. After a breakup, we have to build a new reality

from scratch, and that is frightening. Especially if in previous relationships we existed in a destructive scenario: for example, with an abuser or a partner with addictions. The question arises: "Can I manage on my own? Is it worth trying again?"

What to do?

1.   **Make a firm decision.** Tell yourself, "I have decided. This person is no longer part of my life." This decision requires responsibility because you are rejecting not only him but also the illusions about what your shared future "could have been."

2.   **Spend time alone.** Give yourself time and space to understand: "What exactly am I losing?" Often, a woman misses not the man, but the feeling of being needed, security, the illusion of love. Or the status, comfort, and sex. This is normal. But it is important to understand: All of this can be built with someone else, and most importantly, with yourself.

3.   **Do not rush to "fill the gap" with a new man.** When someone new appears immediately after a breakup, it is often an attempt to avoid pain, not a genuine readiness for love. Moreover, such relationships often develop under the slogan: "Let the ex see what he lost." This is not the path to healing, but a continuation of dependency.

4.   **Allow yourself not to want a relationship.** If you are not ready right now, do not force yourself. But if you feel an inner conflict (like "I do not want a relationship, but somehow I feel so lonely"), it means this is not a choice, but a defense mechanism. And it is worth examining it more deeply.

5.   **Recognize your dependencies.** If you are held by fear of loneliness, financial dependency, or the myth of the "only" man,

this is a reason to work on yourself. Self-confidence, self-sufficiency, financial freedom — these are the keys to true inner freedom.

Saying goodbye to the past is not about "forgetting." It is about "accepting" and letting go. To make room for the new — the alive, the real, the happy.

How do you know that you are moving forward?

- You stop checking on your ex via social media.

- Your thoughts are more focused on the present, not on "what he is doing now."

- You do not start new relationships to "prove" something to someone.

- You begin to breathe easier when you are alone with yourself.

The past has the right to exist. But it should not dictate the terms of your future. By letting go, you make room for your true self. For new love. For real happiness.

Let the future be not just different, but yours. Want to start over? Start with yourself. You deserve love that has no pain.

FALL OUT OF LOVE AND FORGET: AN EFFECTIVE TECHNIQUE TO LET GO OF THE PAST

Falling in love is wonderful, but what do you do when the relationship ends and you cannot forget the person? You miss them, long for them, they continue to appear in your dreams… It is especially difficult if you see them every day — they are your colleague, ex-husband, or, conversely, a married lover. You understand that there is no future, but you cannot let go.

There is a proven, scientifically backed technique that really helps: "Return Emotional Investments." The idea is that when we fall in love, we unconsciously start to "invest" in the person: our love, care, warmth, and soul. These investments form a strong attachment.

We literally "give our soul," "give our heart" — and feel as though part of us left with that person. That is why, even after a breakup, we are drawn to them, we continue to think about them, check their social media, and suffer. Because part of us is with them.

Why does it work? Our brain does not distinguish between imagination and reality. So, it is possible to return our investments mentally, and the effect will be real.

How to do the technique. Find a quiet place. Sit comfortably, close your eyes. Picture the person you want to let go of. Remember what exactly you invested in them: love, warmth, trust, care, hope… Imagine what form these investments could take. For example:

Love — as a wedding ring or a large red heart.

Care—as a soft chair or a huge teddy bear.

Soul—as an angel or a bird.

Mentally take these images back. Feel them returning to you—to your body, your heart, your soul. It is yours, and you have every right to take it back. At this stage, most people feel a rush of energy, relief, and inner calm. It is important: You are not taking someone else's, only your own.

Checking the result. When you mentally say to this person: "Goodbye. I wish you happiness in your personal life"—and nothing inside you flinches, that is a sign: You have let go.

If the phrase causes unpleasant sensations, it means that not everything has been returned yet. Perhaps you are even holding their investments within yourself—then imagine that you are returning their investments to them and taking your own back.

How quickly does the method work? Sometimes the effect is felt immediately—in one meditation. Sometimes it takes 2–3 times doing the practice. But in any case, emotional dependence weakens, and thoughts about the person become rare and neutral.

People often say: "What did I even see in them?"—and this is a sign that you have returned yourself to yourself.

Be careful. The technique really works and can even completely remove sexual attraction. So, use it only when you are absolutely sure you no longer want any kind of relationship with this person—neither emotional nor intimate.

Take care of yourself and remember—you deserve love that also has a place for you.

HOW TO BREAK UP WITH MINIMAL SUFFERING: AN EFFECTIVE STEP-BY-STEP METHOD

Let us say you have been dating a man, everything was going well: pleasant weeks, possibly even months. But then comes the realization that you are no longer on the same path. He is a good person, but not the right one for you. How do you break up in a way that is as gentle as possible for both you and him?

1.   **Prepare for the conversation.** Do not hope that everything will "somehow work out." Think carefully about what you want to say. There will already be plenty of nerves, so it is better to formulate your thoughts in advance.

2.   **Anticipate possible questions.** He might ask, "What happened? What is the issue? Is it because of me?" Think about how you will respond, so that you do not defend yourself, but instead speak honestly and calmly.

3.   **Choose the right time and place.** Avoid holidays or significant dates for both of you. Try to talk in private, in a calm setting where you can be sincere, but still feel safe — for example, in a park.

4.   **Do not delay.** If you have decided to break up, do not drag it out. Waiting just makes everything more difficult. Do not wait for the "right moment." It is better to discuss it as soon as possible.

5.   **Speak in person.** Ideally, in person. If not, by video call. But not via text messages or through someone else. This is important for both you and him.

6.   **Be honest.** Say exactly how you feel. Admit if you are sad or if you regret things. Thank him for the good moments, if there were any. Sincerity makes the breakup easier and cleaner.

7.   **Do not take "breaks."** The conversation must be brought to a close. Do not leave a "comma" and return to the topic in two weeks. This creates different expectations for both of you.

8.   **Do not give in to pleas of "think it over."** If you have made your decision, stick to it. Do not agree to a "break," "one more month," or "what if it gets better" — that will only prolong the pain for both of you.

9.   **Discuss what to do about social media.** Delete? Block? Keep each other as friends but not interact? It is better to agree on this right away to avoid awkwardness and misunderstandings.

Stop communicating for a while and finish up the everyday matters. Even if you decide to "stay friends" — take a pause. It takes time for a new routine to form without him. Return each other's belongings, resolve organizational issues. And stop contact. Do not drag out the "small things," or you will get stuck in the "post-relationship."

Thank him and give yourself time. Say what you are thankful for: the moments, the experience, the feelings. This will help you let go of the relationship with grace and respect. Even if you were the initiator, it is still a loss. Feel the sadness. Be alone. Do not rush into new relationships. Heal.

And remember: A breakup is not always a tragedy. Sometimes it is a step toward your true self.

The end of a relationship is not the end of your story, but the beginning of a new chapter, where you regain your freedom, strength, and inner clarity. By making conscious decisions, letting go of the past, and maintaining self-respect, you create space for real healing and future happiness. Let this journey not be about pain, but about renewal and new horizons.

Dear readers, thank you for taking the time to read this book. I hope it has helped you make sense of your feelings and provided answers to important questions related to love triangles, infidelity, and rebuilding trust in relationships. I am confident that by going through these challenges, you will reach a new level of inner harmony and self-confidence.

If you found this book helpful, I would be grateful for your feedback! Your opinion matters to me and will help other women facing similar situations find the right path. Please leave a review by scanning the QR code below. It will only take a couple of minutes, and it will be incredibly valuable to me.

Thank you for your support and trust!

We appreciate your support, and as a thank you, we are offering audio training sessions to help you activate mental resources and transform reactions, situations, and beliefs.

Get these awesome 4 gifts for free

Gift 1:

The Circle of Power

An exercise that activates the subconscious mind and transforms consciousness, enhancing all the necessary character traits, abilities, and mental states for the swift and effortless realization of any goal.

Gift 2:

10-Minute Transformation Practice for Any Scenario

A simple technique to help you quickly restore balance, manage triggers, and replace negative beliefs with positive ones.

Gift 3:

Emotion Journal for Self-Discovery

A ready-to-use guide for understanding your emotions, reducing stress, and building harmonious relationships. Perfect for daily practice.

Gift 4:

Bonus Guide: "Mental Resources for a Stress-Free Life"

An exercise to help you overcome burnout, manage anxiety, and feel confident in any life situation.

Do not miss the chance to master a technique that will help you better control your emotions and reduce stress!

CONCLUSION

Love is a feeling that brings us joy and happiness, but sometimes it becomes a source of pain and disappointment. When a woman finds herself in a love triangle, facing infidelity and betrayal, her world collapses, and she loses confidence in herself and her relationships. This book has been an attempt to offer you tools that will help you navigate this pain and find a way out of a difficult situation.

We started by analyzing the reasons why men have mistresses and what can be done to avoid infidelity. We explored the importance of a woman's self-esteem and how it affects relationships. We discussed how to raise your self-esteem to become confident and ready for harmonious relationships.

When infidelity has already occurred, it is important to know how to react properly. In the following chapters, we provided strategies to cope with the pain of betrayal, how to survive the first days after infidelity, and what actions to take to avoid losing yourself in this shocking state. We also discussed whether to trust a man when he promises to break up with his mistress and how to overcome the fear that infidelity will happen again.

We did not forget the most painful questions related to forgiveness. Should infidelity be forgiven? When should you leave, and when should you fight for the relationship? How to forgive and restore the family? We addressed all these questions, offering step-by-step instructions and practical recommendations.

Once the decision is made, it is important to know how to learn to trust again, how to strengthen the relationship, and how to avoid mistakes in the future. In the fourth chapter, we suggested strategies for rebuilding trust and examined key rules for healthy relationships. We also did not forget how to properly end a relationship if it no longer has a future. The difficult moments of breaking up and divorce can be painful, but in this book, you will find methods that will help you get through this process with minimal suffering and start a new chapter of your life.

Having gone through all these stages, it is important to remember one thing: Despite all the pain and difficulties, you deserve love, respect, and happiness. This book is not just a guide to surviving love crises but also a path to restoring inner harmony. For every person, after going through trials, can emerge stronger, wiser, and ready to build new, healthy relationships.

Remember, everything depends on you. Your choices, your actions, your ability to forgive and believe — these are the keys that will open the doors to happiness. Do not be afraid of change, be open to new things, and most importantly, do not forget to love yourself. Your relationship with yourself is the first step toward true happiness.

Made in the USA
Monee, IL
30 April 2025

16663363R00100